DID JESUS CONDEMN HOMOSEXUALITY?

Dr. Maxwell Shimba

Printed in the United States of America

SHIMBA
PUBLISHING

TABLE OF CONTENTS

INTRODUCTION

Setting the Context: Why Jesus' View on Homosexuality Matters Today

The question of Jesus' view on homosexuality has become one of the most discussed topics in both religious and cultural discourse. In a time where issues of sexuality, identity, and personal freedom are central to societal change, understanding what Jesus taught—or is believed to have taught—on these matters is crucial for Christians and non-Christians alike. Some contemporary churches and religious leaders argue that Jesus never directly condemned homosexuality, suggesting that His silence implies acceptance or approval. Others believe that His teachings and the broader message of the Bible strongly reinforce a traditional view of sexual morality, including the understanding that marriage and sexual union are meant solely for a man and a woman.

In today's context, where discussions of inclusivity, acceptance, and tolerance are central, examining what Jesus actually said and taught is more relevant than ever. With some denominations endorsing same-sex relationships and ordaining gay clergy, these questions touch the heart of Christian identity, doctrine, and ethics. Christians who hold to the traditional teachings of the Bible feel challenged to uphold their convictions while still extending compassion and respect toward individuals with differing views. This tension can lead to confusion about how to reconcile faith with modern cultural values.

The purpose of this book is to carefully examine Jesus' teachings within the New Testament, as well as the broader biblical context, to determine what can be inferred regarding homosexuality. This exploration is not just about seeking a definitive "yes" or "no" answer; it involves understanding the moral and ethical framework Jesus presented in His teachings. It includes exploring His views on marriage, sexual morality, repentance, and His love for humanity.

For Christians, the authority of Jesus' words is foundational. Jesus is not only seen as a moral teacher but as the embodiment of truth and the Word of God. Therefore, understanding His stance on any moral issue, including homosexuality, is paramount for those who seek to live according to His teachings. However, the complexity of interpreting ancient texts, cultural differences, and translation nuances means that careful examination is required.

Ultimately, this book aims to provide a thorough, respectful, and scripturally grounded examination of this sensitive topic. By doing so, it hopes to clarify Jesus' perspective and offer guidance to those seeking to align their lives with His message in an increasingly complex world. Whether one approaches this subject with a background in faith or from an academic interest, the teachings of Jesus on morality, love, and human relationships remain deeply influential and worthy of sincere exploration.

Objective of the Book: Examining Scriptural Evidence and Theological Principles on Homosexuality

The goal of this book is to approach the question of Jesus' teachings on homosexuality with thoughtful and rigorous analysis. Recognizing that this topic stirs deep emotions and varied opinions, our approach will focus on exploring scriptural evidence within the New Testament and interpreting it through the broader theological principles established by Jesus and His apostles. This exploration seeks not only to clarify whether Jesus directly addressed homosexuality but also to understand His teachings on sexual morality, human relationships, and the sanctity of marriage as they relate to this issue.

Central to this objective is examining how Jesus' recorded words, actions, and His upholding of Hebrew scriptures frame His moral vision. This includes investigating what Jesus affirmed about marriage and human sexuality, His use of terms like *porneia* (often translated as "sexual immorality"), and whether His teachings provide an implicit understanding that guides Christians in contemporary moral and ethical decisions. As Jesus spoke to people within the context of a first-century Jewish culture, where Mosaic Law shaped the moral framework, His approach to the Law's teachings on sexuality, including homosexuality, is essential to understand.

This book also seeks to bridge the principles laid out by Jesus with the teachings of His apostles, particularly Paul, who addressed sexual morality more explicitly in his letters. Since early Christian teaching draws its foundation from Jesus' authority, it is crucial to understand how the apostles' writings reinforce or clarify His moral vision.

Our examination is not merely academic but also seeks to provide clarity and insight for those trying to live out their faith amid modern cultural shifts. Many individuals and churches are seeking answers on how to address this topic with biblical integrity, compassion, and respect. This book aims to offer guidance to those who wish to be true to their faith while engaging with today's diverse perspectives on sexuality and morality.

Ultimately, the objective is to present a balanced, well-researched, and respectful discussion that upholds the importance of Jesus' teachings for today's believers. By grounding our exploration in both scripture and theology, we aim to offer readers a clear understanding of how Jesus and the New Testament address human sexuality, guiding them toward a path that aligns with the principles of love, truth, and holiness central to the Christian faith.

Approach: Differentiating Between Jesus' Explicit Teachings and Broader Biblical Context

In addressing the question of Jesus' perspective on homosexuality, it is essential to approach the topic with a nuanced understanding of how His teachings are recorded in the New Testament and how they interact with the broader biblical context. This book adopts a twofold approach: first, to examine Jesus' explicit statements and actions regarding sexual morality, and second, to interpret His words within the comprehensive framework of biblical teachings, including those presented by His apostles and drawn from the Old Testament.

One of the challenges in discussing Jesus' stance on homosexuality is the lack of direct, explicit statements from Him specifically addressing this topic. As the Gospels record, Jesus did not explicitly mention homosexuality. Some readers interpret this silence as tacit approval or indifference, while others believe that Jesus' teachings on sexual morality implicitly include all forms of sexual behavior outside traditional heterosexual marriage.

To navigate this, our approach clarifies what is directly attributed to Jesus—His recorded words and actions—and distinguishes that from teachings derived from the broader

New Testament, particularly the apostolic letters. For example, while Jesus did not directly address homosexuality, He did emphasize principles about marriage and sexual purity, often reinforcing the teachings of the Hebrew Scriptures. Jesus affirmed the Genesis account of marriage as a union between one man and one woman (Matthew 19:4-6; Mark 10:6-9), which provides an implicit moral vision for human relationships.

The broader biblical context also includes the writings of Paul, who discussed homosexuality directly in several passages. Since early Christians, including Paul, viewed their teachings as extensions of Jesus' message and inspired by the Holy Spirit, these writings contribute to understanding Christian sexual ethics. Paul's letters to the Romans and Corinthians, for example, outline his views on sexual immorality, which included homosexuality (Romans 1:26-27; 1 Corinthians 6:9-11). Thus, these passages are seen by many as essential components of the "Law of Christ" that Jesus' followers are to live by.

By clarifying the distinction between Jesus' direct words and the teachings of the broader biblical context, this book aims to provide a balanced perspective. This approach acknowledges both Jesus' recorded silence on some specifics and the theological continuity established by His apostles. This combined perspective enables a fuller understanding of how Christian beliefs on sexuality developed and guides readers in discerning Jesus' moral framework within the Bible's holistic narrative.

Our aim is to allow readers to make informed interpretations based on scripture, taking into account both the specificity and scope of biblical teachings. In doing so, we seek to offer a respectful and accurate exploration of a challenging subject, providing readers with insights that are both intellectually honest and spiritually grounded.

Meaning of Key Terms

In order to provide a clear and consistent understanding throughout this book, here is a list of key terms frequently used in discussions of sexuality, morality, and biblical teachings. Each term is defined based on its theological, cultural, or biblical context, helping readers to engage more fully with the arguments and perspectives explored in this study.

1. **Homosexuality**: Refers to the romantic or sexual attraction between individuals of the same sex. Within this book, it is explored in relation to biblical teachings on sexual relationships and morality.
2. **Fornication** (*porneia* in Greek)**: A term used throughout the New Testament, often translated as "sexual immorality." *Porneia* is a broad term that includes various forms of illicit sexual conduct, including adultery, fornication, and, by some interpretations, homosexuality. Fornication generally refers to any sexual activity outside the bounds of marriage as traditionally defined in biblical teachings.
3. **Marriage**: In this book, marriage is defined according to the biblical model, presented as a covenantal union between one man and one woman. Jesus referred to this model of marriage when He cited Genesis to affirm God's creation of male and female as partners in marriage (Matthew 19:4-6; Mark 10:6-9).
4. **The Law of Christ**: Refers to the moral and ethical teachings set forth by Jesus and His apostles in the New Testament, especially those teachings that are considered binding on Christians under the New

Covenant established by Jesus. The Law of Christ emphasizes love, grace, and moral transformation, distinguishing it from the Mosaic Law of the Old Testament.

5. **Sodomy**: Derived from the story of Sodom in Genesis 19, this term historically has been associated with homosexual acts, though it also carries broader connotations of moral and sexual depravity in many biblical contexts. The term *sodomites* is used in the Bible to describe those engaging in certain sexual practices considered contrary to God's design.

6. **Repentance**: A central concept in Christian doctrine, repentance involves turning away from sin and dedicating oneself to God. Repentance is often seen as a necessary step for receiving forgiveness and salvation.

7. **Sexual Morality**: Refers to ethical principles and guidelines regarding sexual behavior, as prescribed in both the Old and New Testaments. Sexual morality in the biblical context encompasses purity, fidelity within marriage, and abstention from certain practices such as adultery and fornication.

8. **Apostolic Teachings**: Refers to the writings and instructions of the apostles in the New Testament, particularly those of Paul, Peter, James, and John. These teachings expand on Jesus' message and are seen as authoritative for guiding Christian ethics and doctrine.

9. **Sin**: In Christian theology, sin is any act, thought, or behavior that violates God's law and moral standards. Sin separates individuals from God and requires repentance and redemption through Jesus Christ.

10. **The New Covenant**: The covenant established through Jesus' life, death, and resurrection, which fulfills and replaces the Old Covenant of the Mosaic Law. The New Covenant emphasizes grace, faith in

Christ, and adherence to the moral teachings of the New Testament.

11. **Sexual Immorality**: A broad term for any sexual activity that goes against biblical teachings on holiness and purity. The New Testament frequently uses this term in relation to behaviors that are prohibited under the Law of Christ.

12. **Old Covenant/Law of Moses**: Refers to the covenantal laws given to the Israelites in the Old Testament, including moral, ceremonial, and civil laws. Under the New Covenant, Christians believe that the moral teachings of the Old Covenant inform Christian ethics but that they are no longer bound by the ceremonial and civil requirements.

13. **Red-Letter Teachings**: The words spoken by Jesus, often printed in red in some Bible editions. These teachings are particularly significant as they represent Jesus' direct instructions to His followers.

14. **Holy Spirit**: In Christian doctrine, the Holy Spirit is the third Person of the Trinity, sent by Jesus after His ascension to empower, guide, and convict believers. The Holy Spirit is believed to inspire the apostles' writings and aid believers in understanding and following Jesus' teachings.

15. **Abomination**: A term used in the Bible to denote actions that are detestable or repulsive to God. In the Old Testament, certain behaviors, including specific sexual practices, are labeled as abominations.

16. **Eternal Life**: The Christian belief in life after death with God, made possible through faith in Jesus Christ. Eternal life is a central promise of the New Testament for those who repent and follow Christ.

17. **Holy Scriptures**: Refers to the Bible, considered the inspired Word of God in Christianity. The Holy Scriptures consist of both the Old and New Testaments

and are used as a foundation for Christian doctrine and moral guidance.

18. **Righteousness**: The quality of being morally right or justifiable according to God's standards. In Christian belief, righteousness is granted through faith in Jesus and involves living in a way that aligns with God's will.

19. **Gospel**: Meaning "good news," the Gospel refers to the message of salvation and the teachings of Jesus Christ, particularly regarding His death and resurrection for the forgiveness of sins.

20. **Judgment**: In Christian belief, judgment refers to the final assessment by God of each person's life. Jesus and His apostles taught that individuals would be judged based on their faith and adherence to God's commands.

21. **Salvation**: The deliverance from sin and its consequences, made possible through faith in Jesus Christ. Salvation is seen as a free gift of God's grace and is central to Christian belief.

By defining these terms, this book aims to create a clear and consistent framework for readers. Each term will be used with the same meaning throughout the chapters, allowing for a coherent examination of Jesus' teachings and the broader biblical context on the topic of homosexuality. This foundation also helps readers navigate theological discussions with greater understanding as they engage with the arguments presented in each chapter.

CHAPTER 01

UNDERSTANDING FORNICATION AND BIBLICAL SEXUAL ETHICS

The Meaning of Fornication (**Porneia***)*

To understand biblical teachings on sexuality and whether Jesus condemned homosexuality, it is crucial to begin with the term "fornication," translated from the Greek word *porneia*. This term appears frequently in the New Testament and serves as a foundational concept for understanding sexual ethics in biblical texts.

The Greek Term: Porneia

The word *porneia* derives from the root *porne*, meaning "prostitute" or "harlot," and initially referred to commercialized sexual activity. Over time, its meaning broadened to encompass a wide range of illicit sexual behaviors, including adultery, premarital sex, incest, homosexuality, and bestiality. In biblical contexts, *porneia* refers to any sexual activity outside the bounds of marriage as defined by God—a covenantal union between one man and one woman.

The comprehensive scope of *porneia* is evident in its frequent use throughout the New Testament. For example, in **Matthew 15:19**, Jesus lists fornication alongside other sins such as murder, theft, and false witness, emphasizing its severity. Similarly, in **Galatians 5:19-21**, Paul includes *porneia* in his list of "works of the flesh" that prevent individuals from inheriting the kingdom of God. The term consistently represents behaviors that deviate from God's intended design for human sexuality.

Porneia in Jewish and Greco-Roman Contexts

During the time of Jesus and the early church, Jewish and Greco-Roman societies had distinct views on sexual morality. Jewish teachings, rooted in the Old Testament, strictly prohibited certain sexual acts, including adultery, incest, and homosexual behavior (Leviticus 18:6-22). These prohibitions were considered part of God's moral law and were central to Jewish identity.

In contrast, Greco-Roman culture often celebrated sexual freedom, including practices such as prostitution, pederasty, and same-sex relationships. This cultural backdrop highlights the countercultural stance of Jesus and the apostles, who upheld the sexual ethics of the Hebrew Scriptures and called for sexual purity among believers.

Jesus and the Condemnation of Porneia

While Jesus did not explicitly mention homosexuality, His teachings on *porneia* encompass a broad rejection of all sexual immorality. For example, in **Matthew 5:32**, Jesus speaks against divorce except in cases of *porneia*, implying that any sexual act outside of marriage defiles the marital covenant. Likewise, in **Matthew 19:9**, Jesus reiterates this standard, affirming the sanctity of marriage as a lifelong union between one man and one woman.

Jesus' emphasis on *porneia* as a sin reflects His broader concern for purity and holiness. In **Matthew 15:19**, He declares that *porneia* originates in the heart, linking it to inner corruption and the need for repentance. This understanding aligns with the Old Testament's consistent portrayal of sexual immorality as a sin that separates individuals from God (Leviticus 18:24-30).

The Apostolic Teachings on Porneia

The apostles, inspired by the Holy Spirit, expanded on Jesus' teachings by explicitly addressing various forms of sexual immorality. Paul, in particular, frequently warned against *porneia* in his letters to early Christian communities. For example:

- In **1 Corinthians 6:9-11**, Paul lists homosexual acts alongside other sins such as adultery and idolatry, emphasizing that those who practice such behaviors cannot inherit the kingdom of God unless they repent.
- In **Romans 1:24-27**, Paul describes homosexuality as a result of humanity's rejection of God, calling it a "dishonorable passion" and contrary to nature.
- In **1 Thessalonians 4:3-5**, Paul exhorts believers to abstain from *porneia*, emphasizing that sexual purity is God's will for their sanctification.

These passages demonstrate the continuity between Jesus' teachings on *porneia* and the broader New Testament condemnation of sexual immorality, including homosexuality.

Fornication and the Holiness of Marriage

Central to the biblical concept of *porneia* is the idea that sexual intimacy is reserved for marriage, which is both a divine institution and a reflection of God's relationship with His people. In **Genesis 2:24**, God establishes marriage as a union between one man and one woman, declaring that they shall become "one flesh." This foundational principle underpins the Bible's sexual ethics and defines the boundaries of permissible sexual behavior.

By contrast, *porneia* represents a distortion of God's design for sexuality. Whether through adultery, premarital sex, or same-sex relationships, *porneia* undermines the holiness of marriage and the sanctity of the human body, which is described as a temple of the Holy Spirit (1 Corinthians 6:18-20).

Theological Implications of Porneia

The biblical condemnation of *porneia* reflects God's desire for human flourishing and His call to holiness. Sexual immorality is not merely a violation of divine law; it is also a sin against one's own body and a rejection of God's purpose for human relationships. In **1 Corinthians 6:13**, Paul writes, "The body is not meant for sexual immorality, but for the Lord, and the Lord for the body."

This theological perspective highlights the redemptive power of the Gospel. While *porneia* separates individuals from God, repentance and faith in Jesus Christ offer forgiveness and restoration. In **1 Corinthians 6:11**, Paul reminds believers that some of them were once guilty of *porneia* and other sins, but they were "washed, sanctified, and justified in the name of the Lord Jesus Christ and by the Spirit of our God."

Conclusion

The meaning of *porneia* in the New Testament is both broad and profound, encompassing a range of sexual behaviors that deviate from God's design for marriage and intimacy. Jesus' teachings on *porneia* align with the moral standards of the Old Testament while pointing toward the transformative power of the New Covenant.

By understanding *porneia* and its implications, we gain insight into the biblical call to sexual purity and the sanctity of marriage. This foundation is essential for addressing questions about Jesus' views on homosexuality and for engaging in thoughtful, scripturally grounded discussions on sexual ethics in the modern world.

Understanding Jesus' Perspective on Sexual Morality

Jesus' teachings on sexual ethics form a cornerstone of Christian morality. While Jesus did not explicitly address every possible issue related to sexuality, His broader teachings provide a clear framework for understanding His perspective. By analyzing passages such as **Matthew 15:19**, we can discern the principles that governed His approach to sexual morality and their implications for believers today.

Sexual Morality in Context

The cultural and religious backdrop of Jesus' ministry is essential for interpreting His views on sexual ethics. Jewish society in the first century adhered to the Mosaic Law, which explicitly condemned acts such as adultery, incest, bestiality, and homosexuality (Leviticus 18). These prohibitions were not only moral guidelines but also served to set Israel apart as a holy nation.

Jesus affirmed the validity of these moral laws while simultaneously challenging the superficial legalism of His contemporaries. For Jesus, true obedience to God went beyond external adherence to rules; it required inward purity of heart and mind. This deeper understanding of righteousness is evident in His teachings on sexual ethics.

Matthew 15:19: The Heart of Morality

In **Matthew 15:19**, Jesus declares:

"For out of the heart come evil thoughts, murder, adultery, sexual immorality, theft, false testimony, slander."

This passage highlights several key principles about sin and morality:

1. **The Source of Sin**: Jesus identifies the heart as the origin of sinful behaviors, including "sexual immorality" (*porneia*). This term encompasses a range of sexual sins, such as adultery, fornication, and homosexuality, emphasizing that external actions are rooted in internal corruption.
2. **Equality of Sins**: By listing sexual immorality alongside sins like murder and theft, Jesus underscores

the seriousness of sexual sins. They are not trivial matters but significant violations of God's moral law.
3. **The Call to Purity**: Jesus' focus on the heart reflects His broader teaching that purity begins within. In **Matthew 5:8**, He says, "Blessed are the pure in heart, for they shall see God." Sexual immorality, therefore, is not merely a physical act but a symptom of a defiled heart.

Marriage as the Standard

Jesus consistently upheld marriage as the only context for sexual intimacy. In **Matthew 19:4-6**, He affirms the Genesis account of creation:

"Haven't you read," He replied, "that at the beginning the Creator 'made them male and female,' and said, 'For this reason a man will leave his father and mother and be united to his wife, and the two will become one flesh'? So they are no longer two, but one flesh. Therefore what God has joined together, let no one separate."

This passage reveals several important aspects of Jesus' view on sexual ethics:

1. **Divine Design**: Jesus points to God's creation of male and female as the foundation for human relationships. This design establishes marriage as a lifelong, exclusive union between one man and one woman.
2. **The Sanctity of Marriage**: By quoting Genesis 2:24, Jesus underscores the sacredness of the marital bond. Any sexual activity outside this union, including adultery and homosexuality, deviates from God's original plan.

3. **Unity and Fidelity**: The "one flesh" union signifies not only physical intimacy but also spiritual and emotional oneness. This unity is incompatible with sexual immorality, which fractures relationships and defiles the body.

The Sermon on the Mount: Raising the Standard

In the Sermon on the Mount, Jesus intensifies the demands of the Law by addressing the heart's role in sin. In **Matthew 5:27-28**, He states:

"You have heard that it was said, 'You shall not commit adultery.' But I tell you that anyone who looks at a woman lustfully has already committed adultery with her in his heart."

This teaching expands the definition of sexual immorality in two ways:

1. **Lust as Sin**: Jesus condemns not only physical acts of sexual immorality but also lustful thoughts. This broader standard highlights the importance of internal purity and self-control.
2. **Holistic Obedience**: By addressing the heart, Jesus calls His followers to a higher level of righteousness that exceeds mere rule-following. True discipleship requires aligning one's desires and actions with God's will.

Implications for Homosexuality

While Jesus does not explicitly mention homosexuality in the Gospels, His teachings on sexual immorality and marriage provide a clear framework for evaluating such practices:

1. **Marriage as the Exclusive Context**: Jesus' affirmation of marriage as a union between one man and one woman excludes same-sex relationships. By defining marriage in terms of male and female, He upholds the biblical view of sexuality as complementary and procreative.
2. **The Scope of *Porneia***: As discussed earlier, *porneia* encompasses all forms of sexual immorality, including homosexuality. By condemning *porneia*, Jesus implicitly rejects any sexual behavior outside the bounds of heterosexual marriage.
3. **The Call to Repentance**: Jesus' mission was to call sinners to repentance and transformation. In **John 8:11**, He tells the woman caught in adultery, "Go now and leave your life of sin." This command applies to all forms of sexual immorality, including homosexuality, underscoring the need for repentance and obedience to God's Word.

Practical Applications

Jesus' teachings on sexual ethics challenge believers to:

1. **Pursue Holiness**: Sexual purity is not merely about avoiding certain behaviors; it requires cultivating a heart that honors God in thought, word, and deed.
2. **Honor Marriage**: By upholding the sanctity of marriage, Christians can reflect God's design for human relationships and provide a countercultural witness in a world that often devalues commitment and fidelity.
3. **Extend Grace and Truth**: While Jesus condemned sin, He also offered forgiveness and restoration to those who repented. Believers are called to follow His

example by speaking the truth in love and extending grace to those struggling with sexual immorality.

Conclusion

Jesus' teachings on sexual ethics, as seen in passages like **Matthew 15:19**, provide a comprehensive framework for understanding His perspective on morality. By emphasizing the heart's role in sin, affirming the sanctity of marriage, and calling for repentance, Jesus sets a high standard for His followers.

These principles not only clarify Jesus' view on sexual immorality but also equip believers to navigate contemporary debates on issues such as homosexuality with grace, wisdom, and fidelity to Scripture.

Thayer's Lexicon and Biblical Usage of *Porneia*

A Scholarly Exploration of Illicit Sexuality in the Bible

The Greek word *porneia* holds a central place in biblical discussions of sexual immorality. Found in numerous passages throughout the New Testament, it broadly refers to illicit sexual acts that deviate from God's intended design for human relationships. By examining *porneia* through the lens of **Thayer's Greek Lexicon** and the interpretations of biblical scholars, we can better understand its application to various forms of sexual misconduct, including homosexuality.

Understanding Porneia *in the Greek Lexicon*

Thayer's Greek Lexicon defines *porneia* as:

"Illicit sexual intercourse; adultery, fornication, homosexuality, lesbianism, intercourse with animals, etc."

This definition highlights several critical points:

1. **Broad Scope**: *Porneia* encompasses a wide range of sexual behaviors considered sinful according to biblical standards. It is not limited to fornication (sex outside of marriage) but includes acts like adultery, homosexuality, and bestiality.
2. **Illicit Nature**: The term specifically refers to acts that violate God's moral law. This illicit nature makes *porneia* distinct from the sexual relationship within the confines of marriage, which the Bible upholds as holy and pure (Hebrews 13:4).
3. **Cultural Relevance**: In the Greco-Roman world, *porneia* was used to describe behaviors that were often normalized in society but condemned by Scripture. Understanding this context helps clarify why the New Testament repeatedly warns against it.

Biblical Usage of Porneia

The New Testament uses *porneia* extensively to address issues of sexual immorality. Key passages include:

- **Matthew 15:19**:

  "For out of the heart come evil thoughts, murder, adultery, sexual immorality (*porneia*), theft, false testimony, slander."

Here, Jesus categorizes *porneia* as a sin originating from the heart. This aligns with His broader teaching that internal purity is as important as external actions (Matthew 5:28).

- **1 Corinthians 6:18**:

"Flee from sexual immorality (*porneia*). All other sins a person commits are outside the body, but whoever sins sexually sins against their own body."

Paul emphasizes the unique nature of sexual sin, which defiles not only the spirit but also the physical body.

- **Galatians 5:19-21**:

"The acts of the flesh are obvious: sexual immorality (*porneia*), impurity and debauchery; idolatry and witchcraft; hatred, discord, jealousy, fits of rage, selfish ambition, dissensions, factions and envy; drunkenness, orgies, and the like. I warn you, as I did before, that those who live like this will not inherit the kingdom of God."

Here, *porneia* is listed among other sins that disqualify individuals from God's kingdom. This underscores its seriousness in Christian ethics.

Thayer's Analysis: Specific Forms of Porneia

According to Thayer's Lexicon, *porneia* includes the following categories:

1. **Adultery** (*moicheia*): The violation of the marriage covenant through sexual relations with someone other

than one's spouse. This is explicitly condemned in both the Old and New Testaments (Exodus 20:14; Matthew 5:27-28).

2. **Fornication**: Sexual relations outside of marriage, including premarital and extramarital affairs. This is a common application of *porneia* in passages like 1 Corinthians 7:2.

3. **Homosexuality and Lesbianism**: These practices fall under the umbrella of *porneia*, as evidenced by Paul's writings in Romans 1:26-27 and 1 Corinthians 6:9-10, which explicitly condemn same-sex relations.

4. **Bestiality**: Intercourse with animals, which is explicitly prohibited in Leviticus 18:23 and classified as an abomination under God's law.

5. **Prostitution**: The root word of *porneia* (from *pornē*, meaning "prostitute") indicates that any involvement in prostitution, whether as a participant or a client, constitutes sexual immorality (1 Corinthians 6:15-16).

Scholarly Interpretations of Porneia

Biblical scholars generally agree that *porneia* serves as a comprehensive term for all forms of sexual sin. Some notable interpretations include:

- **William Barclay**: In his commentary on the New Testament, Barclay states that *porneia* represents "all sexual activity outside the sanctity of marriage." This broad definition aligns with the traditional Christian understanding of sexual purity.

- **Leon Morris**: Morris emphasizes that *porneia* includes acts that degrade the body and dishonor God's intention for human relationships. He argues that this term challenges cultural norms that seek to normalize immoral behaviors.

- **Craig L. Blomberg**: Blomberg notes that *porneia* serves as a warning against the permissiveness of the Greco-Roman world, where behaviors like homosexuality and adultery were often accepted. He stresses that Christians are called to a higher standard of holiness.

Implications for Christian Ethics

The comprehensive nature of *porneia* in biblical usage has significant implications for Christian sexual ethics:

1. **Holistic Morality**: *Porneia* challenges believers to uphold purity not only in their actions but also in their thoughts and intentions. This holistic approach reflects Jesus' teaching in Matthew 5:27-28.
2. **Marriage as the Boundary**: By defining sexual immorality as anything outside the bounds of heterosexual marriage, *porneia* affirms the sanctity of the marital union.
3. **Rejection of Cultural Relativism**: The Bible's condemnation of *porneia* serves as a countercultural statement, calling Christians to resist societal pressures that normalize sexual sin.

Conclusion

The term *porneia*, as defined by Thayer's Lexicon and interpreted by biblical scholars, provides a comprehensive framework for understanding sexual immorality in Scripture. Its inclusion of practices like adultery, fornication, homosexuality, and prostitution underscores the seriousness with which the Bible treats these issues.

By examining *porneia* through its lexical and biblical usage, believers can gain a clearer understanding of God's design for human sexuality. This understanding equips Christians to navigate contemporary moral challenges with faithfulness to Scripture and a commitment to holiness.

CHAPTER 02

MARRIAGE ACCORDING TO JESUS

Marriage is one of the foundational institutions established by God, and Jesus' teachings on this subject are essential for understanding His perspective on sexual morality. In passages such as Matthew 19:3-9 and Mark 10:6-8, Jesus not only affirmed the sanctity of marriage but also defined it as a union between one man and one woman. This chapter provides an expository study of these texts, enriched by references to exhaustive Strong's Concordance and related biblical scholarship.

Jesus and the Institution of Marriage

Jesus' teachings on marriage were grounded in God's original design, as revealed in Genesis. When confronted by Pharisees about the topic of divorce, Jesus pointed back to creation to affirm God's intent for marriage.

Key Text: Matthew 19:3-9

"Some Pharisees came to Him to test Him. They asked, 'Is it lawful for a man to divorce his wife for any and every reason?' 'Haven't you read,' He replied, 'that at the beginning the Creator "made them male and female," and said, "For this reason a man will leave his father and mother and be united to his wife, and the two will become one flesh"? So they are no longer two, but one flesh. Therefore, what God has joined together, let no one separate.'" *(Matthew 19:3-6, NIV)*

This passage encapsulates several key principles of Jesus' view on marriage:

1. **Creation as the Foundation** Jesus cites Genesis 1:27 (*"God created them male and female"*) and Genesis 2:24 (*"the two will become one flesh"*) to highlight that marriage was divinely instituted. The phrase *"male and female"* (Strong's G730 and G2338) underscores the complementarity of genders in God's design.

2. **Unity in Marriage** The concept of becoming *"one flesh"* (Greek: *sarx mia*, Strong's G4561) signifies a deep physical, emotional, and spiritual bond between a husband and wife. This unity reflects God's purpose for intimacy and procreation within the boundaries of marriage.

3. **Permanence of Marriage** Jesus declares that marriage is a lifelong covenant: *"What God has joined together, let no one separate."* The Greek verb for *"joined together"* (*syzeugnymi*, Strong's G4801) conveys the idea of an unbreakable bond.

Key Text: Mark 10:6-8

"But at the beginning of creation God 'made them male and female.' 'For this reason a man will leave his father and mother and be united to his wife, and the two will become one flesh.' So they are no longer two, but one flesh." (Mark 10:6-8, NIV)

This parallel account reiterates Jesus' emphasis on marriage as a union between one man and one woman, rooted in creation. The use of *"beginning"* (Greek: *arche*, Strong's G746) reinforces the timelessness of God's marital design.

The Complementary Design of Male and Female

In both passages, Jesus emphasizes that marriage is between *"male"* (Greek: *arsen*, Strong's G730) and *"female"* (Greek: *thelys*, Strong's G2338). This complementarity is foundational to the biblical concept of marriage.

1. **Biological Complementarity** The physical differences between male and female reflect God's design for reproduction and family building. Genesis 1:28 commands Adam and Eve to *"be fruitful and multiply,"* a mandate that is inherently tied to their biological complementarity.

2. **Spiritual Union** Beyond the physical, marriage symbolizes a spiritual partnership where husband and wife support and sanctify one another. Paul later expands on this idea in Ephesians 5:31-33, comparing the marital relationship to Christ's relationship with the Church.

Jesus' Rejection of Divorce and Sexual Immorality

Jesus also addressed the topic of divorce in the context of marriage, linking it to sexual morality.

Matthew 19:9

"I tell you that anyone who divorces his wife, except for sexual immorality (porneia), and marries another woman commits adultery."

1. **Exception Clause** The phrase *"except for sexual immorality"* (Greek: *porneia*, Strong's G4202) signifies that divorce is permissible only in cases of severe marital infidelity. This reinforces the sanctity of marriage by limiting grounds for dissolution.
2. **Adultery as a Consequence** Jesus highlights that remarriage after an unjust divorce constitutes adultery (Greek: *moicheia*, Strong's G3431). This underscores the gravity of breaking the marital covenant.

Theological Implications of Jesus' Teachings

1. **Marriage as a Reflection of God's Covenant** In defining marriage as a lifelong union, Jesus reflects

God's covenantal faithfulness. Just as God remains faithful to His people, spouses are called to remain faithful to each other.

2. **Exclusivity of Heterosexual Marriage** By affirming the Genesis creation account, Jesus implicitly excludes all other forms of union, including same-sex relationships. His teaching leaves no room for redefining marriage beyond its original design.

3. **Sexual Morality and Holiness** Jesus connects marriage with sexual purity. By condemning *porneia*, He calls believers to uphold God's standards of holiness in their relationships.

Expository Insights from Strong's Concordance

1. *"Made"* (Greek: *poieo*, Strong's G4160): Indicates God's intentional act in creating male and female, highlighting the deliberate nature of His design.

2. *"United"* (Greek: *kollao*, Strong's G2853): Suggests a binding together, emphasizing the permanence of the marital bond.

3. *"One Flesh"* (Greek: *sarx mia*, Strong's G4561): Represents the profound unity that marriage creates, transcending physical union to include emotional and spiritual oneness.

Conclusion

Jesus' teachings on marriage, as presented in Matthew 19 and Mark 10, reaffirm the sanctity, exclusivity, and permanence of the marital union between one man and one woman. By grounding His teachings in the creation account, Jesus emphasizes that marriage is not a human construct but a divine institution.

For Christians, these teachings provide a clear framework for understanding sexual morality and resisting cultural pressures to redefine marriage. As followers of Christ, we are called to honor God's original design, striving for holiness in all aspects of our lives, including our relationships.

The "One Flesh" Union

Marriage, as ordained by God, is characterized by the concept of a "one flesh" union. This profound phrase, first introduced in Genesis 2:24 and reaffirmed by Jesus in the New Testament, encapsulates the theological and relational significance of marriage. It highlights not only the physical unity of a husband and wife but also their emotional, spiritual, and covenantal oneness. This chapter explores the theological depth of the "one flesh" union, its implications for marriage, and the sacredness it bestows on the marital bond.

Biblical Foundation of the "One Flesh" Union

The phrase "one flesh" originates in the creation narrative:

"Therefore a man shall leave his father and mother and be joined to his wife, and they shall become one flesh." (Genesis 2:24, NKJV)

Jesus reiterates this in His teachings on marriage:

"For this reason a man will leave his father and mother and be united to his wife, and the two will become one flesh. So

they are no longer two, but one flesh. Therefore what God has joined together, let no one separate." *(Matthew 19:5-6, NIV; cf. Mark 10:7-9)*

1. **"Leave" (Hebrew: עָזַב, `azab; Strong's H5800)** The term implies a deliberate departure or forsaking of previous ties to form a new and primary relationship. In marriage, this denotes prioritizing the marital bond over familial ties.

2. **"Be Joined" (Hebrew: דָּבַק, dabaq; Strong's H1692)** Often translated as "cleave," this term conveys the idea of sticking or adhering firmly, symbolizing the enduring commitment between husband and wife. In Greek (Matthew 19:5), the equivalent term is *kollao* (Strong's G2853), meaning "to glue or unite closely."

3. **"One Flesh" (Hebrew: בָּשָׂר אֶחָד, basar echad; Strong's H1320 & H259)** The Hebrew words *basar* (flesh) and *echad* (one) together signify a profound union. This phrase goes beyond physical intimacy to encompass a holistic unity—physical, emotional, and spiritual.

Theological Significance of "One Flesh"

1. **Sacred Covenant** The "one flesh" union reflects the sacred covenantal nature of marriage. Just as God's covenant with His people is characterized by faithfulness and permanence, so too is the marital covenant. This is why Jesus declared:

"What God has joined together, let no one separate." (Matthew 19:6)

The divine joining (*syzeugnymi*, Strong's G4801) signifies that marriage is not merely a human contract but a God-ordained bond.

2. **Unity and Complementarity** The union of "one flesh" represents the complementary design of male and female. Each brings unique strengths and qualities to the relationship, fulfilling God's purpose for marriage as a partnership. Genesis 1:27 states:

   "So God created mankind in His own image, in the image of God He created them; male and female He created them."

   This complementarity allows the couple to fulfill the command to "be fruitful and multiply" (Genesis 1:28).

3. **Symbol of Christ and the Church** Paul deepens the theological meaning of "one flesh" in Ephesians 5:31-32, where he compares the marital union to the relationship between Christ and the Church:

   "For this reason a man will leave his father and mother and be united to his wife, and the two will become one flesh. This is a profound mystery—but I am talking about Christ and the Church."

   Marriage, therefore, serves as a living parable of Christ's sacrificial love and the Church's faithful response.

Implications of the "One Flesh" Union for Marriage

1. **Permanence of Marriage** The "one flesh" union underscores the indissolubility of marriage. Jesus' statement, *"What God has joined together, let no one separate"* (Matthew 19:6), affirms that marriage is meant to be a lifelong commitment. Divorce, except in cases of unfaithfulness (*porneia*), disrupts this sacred union (Matthew 19:9).

2. **Sexual Purity and Exclusivity** The physical aspect of the "one flesh" union emphasizes the exclusivity of sexual intimacy within marriage. Paul writes in 1 Corinthians 6:16-18:

   "Do you not know that he who unites himself with a prostitute is one with her in body? For it is said, 'The two will become one flesh.' But whoever is united with the Lord is one with Him in spirit. Flee from sexual immorality."

   This passage warns against sexual immorality (*porneia*, Strong's G4202), which violates the sanctity of the marital bond.

3. **Shared Responsibility** The "one flesh" union implies a shared life, where husband and wife bear each other's burdens and work together toward mutual goals. Ecclesiastes 4:9-12 illustrates the strength of partnership, declaring, *"Two are better than one."*

4. **Procreation and Family Building** The union facilitates the creation of new life, fulfilling God's command in Genesis 1:28. Children born within this union are seen as blessings, reinforcing the generational continuity of God's covenant.

Expository Insights from Strong's Concordance

1. *"Flesh"* (Greek: *sarx*, Strong's G4561): In biblical usage, this term can refer to the physical body, human nature, or relational unity. In the context of marriage, it symbolizes the holistic bond between husband and wife.
2. *"One"* (Greek: *heis*, Strong's G1520): Denotes unity or singularity, emphasizing the inseparability of the marital bond.
3. *"Joined"* (Greek: *kollao*, Strong's G2853): Implies a close, permanent bond, akin to being glued together.

Conclusion

The "one flesh" union is central to the biblical understanding of marriage. It represents the holistic unity of husband and wife, reflecting God's covenantal love and His design for human relationships. Through this sacred bond, couples are called to live in faithfulness, purity, and mutual support, serving as a testament to God's purpose for humanity.

As Jesus affirmed in His teachings, the "one flesh" union is not merely a physical or emotional connection but a divine mystery that points to the greater reality of Christ's love for the Church. Recognizing the sacredness of this union challenges believers to uphold the sanctity of marriage in a world that often seeks to redefine it.

The Creation Ordinance

The "Creation Ordinance" refers to the divine principles established by God during the creation of the world, including the institution of marriage. Jesus, as the Creator (John 1:3), holds a central role in defining and affirming these ordinances. This chapter explores the theological implications of Jesus as the Creator and His establishment of the first marriage between Adam and Eve. Through a comprehensive examination of scriptural texts and insights from Strong's Concordance, we delve into the timeless truths about marriage as ordained by God.

Jesus as Creator: A Foundational Truth

The Gospel of John reveals Jesus' role in creation:

"All things were made through Him, and without Him nothing was made that was made." (John 1:3, NKJV)

The Greek word for "made" is *ginomai* (Strong's G1096), meaning "to come into existence" or "to be created." This verse establishes Jesus as the divine agent through whom all creation, including the institution of marriage, was brought into being.

Paul affirms this in Colossians 1:16:

"For by Him all things were created that are in heaven and that are on earth, visible and invisible, whether thrones or dominions or principalities or powers. All things were created through Him and for Him."

The First Marriage: Adam and Eve

The first marriage, described in Genesis 2:18-24, serves as the prototype for all future unions. This passage emphasizes the complementary nature of man and woman and the sanctity of their union:

"And the LORD God said, 'It is not good that man should be alone; I will make him a helper comparable to him.'" (Genesis 2:18, NKJV)

1. **"Helper Comparable"**
   - *Helper* (Hebrew: עֵזֶר, *ezer*; Strong's H5828): This term signifies one who provides essential support. It does not imply inferiority but highlights the complementary relationship between man and woman.
   - *Comparable* (Hebrew: כְּנֶגְדּוֹ, *kenegdo*; Strong's H5048): Translated as "suitable," it denotes harmony and equality in the relationship.
2. **Creation of Woman**

   "Then the rib which the LORD God had taken from man He made into a woman, and He brought her to the man." (Genesis 2:22)

   - *Rib* (Hebrew: צֵלָע, *tsela*; Strong's H6763): Symbolizes shared essence and equality, as the woman was formed from the man's own body.
3. **Union in Marriage**

   "Therefore a man shall leave his father and mother and be joined to his wife, and they shall become one flesh." (Genesis 2:24)

- o *Leave* (Hebrew: עָזַב, *azab*; Strong's H5800): Indicates a shift in primary allegiance, prioritizing the marital bond.
- o *Be Joined* (Hebrew: דָּבַק, *dabaq*; Strong's H1692): Implies a deep, permanent attachment.

Theological Implications of Creation Ordinance

1. **Marriage as a Divine Institution** Marriage is not a human invention but a divine ordinance established by Jesus as Creator. This is affirmed by Jesus in Matthew 19:4-6:

   "Have you not read that He who made them at the beginning 'made them male and female,' and said, 'For this reason a man shall leave his father and mother and be joined to his wife, and the two shall become one flesh'? So then, they are no longer two but one flesh. Therefore what God has joined together, let not man separate."

   - o *Made* (Greek: *ktizo*, Strong's G2936): Indicates intentional creation with purpose.
   - o *Joined* (Greek: *syzeugnymi*, Strong's G4801): Describes God's active role in uniting husband and wife.

2. **Complementarity of Genders** The creation of man and woman underscores their complementary roles. Together, they reflect the image of God:

   "So God created man in His own image; in the image of God He created him; male and female He created them." (Genesis 1:27)

The term "male and female" (Hebrew: זָכָר וּנְקֵבָה, *zakar* and *neqebah*) highlights their biological and functional distinctiveness, designed for unity and procreation.

3. **Sanctity of the "One Flesh" Union** The "one flesh" union signifies more than physical intimacy; it represents emotional, spiritual, and covenantal unity. Jesus' reaffirmation of this concept in Matthew 19:6 emphasizes its sacredness and permanence.
4. **Marriage as a Reflection of Divine Relationships** Paul expounds on the symbolic nature of marriage in Ephesians 5:31-32, where he compares the marital bond to the relationship between Christ and the Church. This theological parallel elevates marriage to a reflection of divine love and commitment.

Comprehensive Commentary

1. **God's Sovereignty in Marriage** By establishing marriage at creation, God demonstrated His sovereign authority over human relationships. Marriage, therefore, is not subject to cultural redefinition but remains rooted in divine purpose.
2. **Marriage and Human Flourishing** The creation ordinance of marriage provides a framework for human flourishing. It fosters companionship, mutual support, and the continuation of humanity through procreation.
3. **Jesus' Affirmation of Creation Principles** Jesus' teachings on marriage consistently point back to the creation ordinance. His reference to Genesis 1:27 and 2:24 in Matthew 19 underscores His approval of the

original design for marriage as a union between one man and one woman.

4. **Permanence and Exclusivity** The creation ordinance establishes marriage as a lifelong and exclusive bond. This counters modern notions of casual or temporary relationships, reaffirming the sacredness of marital commitment.

Conclusion

The creation ordinance, established by Jesus as Creator, lays the foundation for the biblical understanding of marriage. It defines marriage as a sacred, exclusive, and permanent union between one man and one woman. By reaffirming this ordinance, Jesus not only validated its relevance but also highlighted its theological significance as a reflection of divine love and purpose.

As followers of Christ, embracing and upholding the creation ordinance is a vital expression of faithfulness to God's design and intent for humanity.

CHAPTER 03

THE MOSAIC LAW AND HOMOSEXUALITY

The Law of Moses on Homosexuality: An Analysis of Leviticus 18:22

The Mosaic Law contains explicit commandments addressing human behavior, morality, and holiness. Among these laws, Leviticus 18:22 provides a clear prohibition against homosexual acts, designating them as an "abomination." This chapter explores the historical, theological, and moral implications of this verse, using exhaustive references from Strong's Concordance and a comprehensive commentary.

Leviticus 18:22: The Prohibition Explained

"You shall not lie with a male as with a woman; it is an abomination." (Leviticus 18:22, NKJV)

1. **Key Terms and Their Meaning**
   - **"Lie"** (*shakab*, שָׁכַב; Strong's H7901):* This term refers to sexual intercourse and is used throughout the Old Testament to denote both consensual and non-consensual sexual relations. Its usage in this context specifically addresses consensual homosexual acts.
   - **"Male"** (*zakar*, זָכָר; Strong's H2145):* This term signifies the biological male gender, leaving no ambiguity about the subject of the command.
   - **"As with a woman"** (*ishshah*, אִשָּׁה; Strong's H802):* This phrase emphasizes the prohibition of treating a male as a female in the context of sexual relations, rejecting any distortion of natural sexual roles.
   - **"Abomination"** (*toebah*, תּוֹעֵבָה; Strong's H8441):* Defined as something detestable or repugnant, this term is often used in the context of moral and ritual purity laws, reflecting God's holiness and moral standards.

Historical and Cultural Context

The prohibition in Leviticus 18:22 is part of a larger section of the Mosaic Law that addresses sexual ethics and the sanctity of human relationships (Leviticus 18:1-30). These laws were given to the Israelites as they prepared to enter Canaan, a land where many of the prohibited practices were common among pagan cultures.

1. **Canaanite Practices** Archaeological and historical evidence suggests that homosexual acts, along with other forms of sexual immorality, were prevalent in Canaanite worship and daily life. The Mosaic Law's prohibition served to distinguish Israel as a holy people, separate from the surrounding nations.
2. **Holiness and Covenant Identity**
   - Leviticus 18:3: *"You shall not do as they do in the land of Egypt, where you lived, and you shall not do as they do in the land of Canaan, to which I am bringing   you."*
     This verse establishes the call for Israel to reflect God's holiness by rejecting the moral depravity of other cultures.

Theological Significance

1. **God's Moral Character** The designation of homosexual acts as an abomination reflects the moral purity and holiness of God.
   - Leviticus 19:2: *"You shall be holy, for I the LORD your God am holy."*
   - The term "holy" (*qadosh*, קָדוֹשׁ; Strong's H6918) signifies being set apart and morally pure, aligning with God's own character.
2. **Natural Order and Creation Design** The prohibition upholds the natural order established at creation, as seen in Genesis 1:27-28:

   "So God created man in His own image; in the image of God He created him; male and female He created them. Then God blessed them, and God said to them, 'Be fruitful and multiply.'"

- o The complementary design of male and female in procreation and union reflects God's intent for human relationships. Homosexual acts, by their nature, deviate from this design.

3. **Abomination and Divine Justice** The term *toebah* (abomination) carries a strong moral judgment, indicating actions that violate the divine order. It is used elsewhere in the Mosaic Law to describe idolatry (Deuteronomy 7:25), false worship (Deuteronomy 12:31), and other grave sins.

Consequences of Disobedience

1. **Sodom and Gomorrah as an Example** Leviticus 18:22 echoes the judgment pronounced on Sodom and Gomorrah (Genesis 19:4-11), cities destroyed for their sexual immorality, including homosexual acts. Jude 1:7 reiterates their fate:

   "As Sodom and Gomorrah, and the cities around them in a similar manner to these, having given themselves over to sexual immorality and gone after strange flesh, are set forth as an example, suffering the vengeance of eternal fire."

2. **The Land and Its Purity** Leviticus 18:25 warns that the land itself becomes defiled by such acts:

   "For the land is defiled; therefore I visit the punishment of its iniquity upon it, and the land vomits out its inhabitants."

This underscores the communal consequences of individual immorality, as sin impacts both society and the environment.

Comprehensive Commentary

1. **Universal Moral Principles** Although the Mosaic Law was given to Israel, its moral principles reflect universal truths about human relationships and God's design. The prohibition against homosexuality is reiterated in the New Testament, affirming its continued relevance (Romans 1:24-27, 1 Corinthians 6:9-10).
2. **Holiness in Action** Leviticus 18 emphasizes holiness in all areas of life, including sexuality. The call to holiness requires obedience to God's commands, rejecting cultural norms that conflict with divine law.
3. **Redemptive Hope** While Leviticus 18:22 highlights the severity of sin, the broader biblical narrative points to redemption through Christ. 1 Corinthians 6:11 offers hope for those who repent:

"And such were some of you. But you were washed, but you were sanctified, but you were justified in the name of the Lord Jesus and by the Spirit of our God."

Conclusion

Leviticus 18:22 provides a clear and unequivocal prohibition against homosexual acts, rooted in God's moral character and creation design. The designation of such acts as an abomination underscores their seriousness and the need for holiness in all aspects of life.

As part of the Mosaic Law, this command served to set Israel apart as a holy nation. Its moral principles, however, continue to inform Christian ethics today, affirming the sanctity of marriage and human sexuality as designed by God. Through Christ, believers are called to uphold these principles while extending grace and redemption to those who repent.

Sodom and Gomorrah

Examining the Story of Sodom and Its Lessons on Sexual Immorality

The story of Sodom and Gomorrah, as recorded in Genesis 19, serves as one of the most vivid examples of divine judgment in the Bible. This narrative has been interpreted throughout Jewish and Christian traditions as a caution against various forms of immorality, particularly sexual immorality. This chapter provides a comprehensive study of the text, using an expository approach with references and an exhaustive analysis using Strong's Concordance.

The Narrative of Sodom and Gomorrah (Genesis 19)

The Key Passage

"Now before they lay down, the men of the city, the men of Sodom, both old and young, all the people from every quarter, surrounded the house. And they called to Lot and said to him, 'Where are the men who came to you tonight? Bring them out to us that we may know them carnally.'" (Genesis 19:4-5, NKJV)

1. **"Know them carnally"**
   o **"Know"** (*yada'*, יָדַע; Strong's H3045):* While often used to mean general knowledge, *yada'* in this context implies sexual relations, as seen in passages like Genesis 4:1 (*"Adam knew Eve his wife, and she conceived"*).
   o The phrase indicates the men of Sodom intended to engage in homosexual acts with Lot's visitors, reflecting widespread moral corruption.
2. **Lot's Response** Lot's refusal to surrender his guests reveals his recognition of the gravity of their intentions. He pleads with the men of Sodom, calling their behavior *wickedness* (*ra'ah*, רָעָה; Strong's H7451). This term underscores the moral depravity of their actions.

Theological and Moral Themes

1. The Sin of Sodom

The sin of Sodom is multifaceted, encompassing sexual immorality, arrogance, and neglect of the needy.

- **Sexual Immorality**: Jude 1:7 highlights their pursuit of *"strange flesh"* (*heteras sarkos*, ἕτερας σάρκος; Strong's G2087, G4561), referring to unnatural sexual desires, specifically homosexual acts.

- **Injustice and Oppression**: Ezekiel 16:49-50 broadens the scope, identifying pride, idleness, and neglect of the poor as additional sins:

  "Look, this was the iniquity of your sister Sodom: She and her daughter had pride, fullness of food, and abundance of idleness; neither did she strengthen the hand of the poor and needy."

2. Divine Judgment and Mercy

- God's judgment on Sodom demonstrates His intolerance of unrepentant sin. Genesis 19:24 describes the destruction:

  "Then the Lord rained brimstone and fire on Sodom and Gomorrah, from the Lord out of the heavens."

- However, God's willingness to save Lot and his family reflects His mercy toward the righteous, aligning with Abraham's intercession in Genesis 18:23-33.

Interpretation in Jewish Tradition

1. **Talmudic Insights** Jewish rabbinical writings emphasize Sodom's lack of hospitality and justice. The *Midrash* describes Sodomites as oppressing strangers and practicing extreme selfishness, underscoring the societal breakdown beyond sexual immorality.
2. **Moral Lessons**
   - The Jewish understanding often views Sodom as a warning against collective societal sins, including greed and neglect of the vulnerable.

- o The story serves as a call to uphold justice and compassion, central values in Jewish ethics.

Interpretation in Christian Tradition

1. **New Testament References**
   - o **Jude 1:7**: The New Testament confirms sexual immorality as a key aspect of Sodom's sin:

     "As Sodom and Gomorrah, and the cities around them in a similar manner to these, having given themselves over to sexual immorality and gone after strange flesh, are set forth as an example, suffering the vengeance of eternal fire."

   - o **2 Peter 2:6-7**: Sodom is portrayed as an example of God's judgment on the ungodly, emphasizing Lot's righteousness in contrast to the city's wickedness.
2. **Moral and Eschatological Lessons**
   - o The destruction of Sodom becomes a symbol of divine judgment against sin, with implications for the final judgment (Matthew 10:15, Luke 17:28-30).
   - o The narrative also underscores the responsibility of believers to live righteously amidst a corrupt society.

Strong's Concordance: Key Word Study

Sodom (סְדֹם; Strong's H5467)

- Meaning: *"Burnt"* or *"Scorching"*.
- The name itself reflects the fiery judgment that befell the city.

Abomination (תּוֹעֵבָה; Strong's H8441)

- The term is often used to describe acts that are morally detestable to God, including sexual immorality and idolatry (Leviticus 18:22, Deuteronomy 7:25).

Judgment (שָׁפַט; Strong's H8199)

- Meaning: To judge or govern. God's judgment on Sodom serves as an archetype of divine justice.

Expository Commentary

1. **Moral Decline and Societal Corruption** Sodom represents the extreme consequences of unrestrained sin. The lack of moral boundaries led to a society where even the sanctity of guests was violated, a direct affront to God's design for human relationships.
2. **The Call to Righteousness** Lot's preservation highlights the principle that God spares the righteous while judging the wicked. This foreshadows the redemption available through Christ for those who repent and turn to God.
3. **Universal Relevance**
   - The story transcends its historical context, offering a timeless warning against societal and individual sin.
   - It emphasizes the need for vigilance, compassion, and faithfulness in a world prone to moral decay.

Conclusion

The story of Sodom and Gomorrah serves as a stark reminder of the consequences of unchecked sin. It underscores God's justice in condemning immorality and His mercy in delivering the righteous. Both Jewish and Christian traditions view this narrative as a call to uphold moral integrity and compassion.

Through the lens of biblical theology, the account challenges believers to reflect God's holiness in their lives, standing firm against cultural pressures while extending grace and truth to a fallen world.

Transition to the Law of Christ

How Jesus' Ministry Under the Mosaic Law Set the Stage for a New Covenant

Jesus Christ's ministry unfolded within the framework of the Mosaic Law, yet it also laid the foundation for a transformative new covenant. This chapter explores the theological transition from the Law of Moses to the Law of Christ, using an expository approach and a detailed study with Strong's Concordance.

Jesus' Ministry Under the Mosaic Law

Understanding the Mosaic Law

The Mosaic Law, given to Israel at Mount Sinai, served as the covenantal framework between God and His people (Exodus 19:5-6). This law encompassed moral, ceremonial, and civil codes:

1. **Moral Law**: Commands such as the Ten Commandments (Exodus 20).
2. **Ceremonial Law**: Rituals and sacrifices to maintain purity and atone for sin (Leviticus 1-7).
3. **Civil Law**: Regulations governing societal conduct (Deuteronomy 24).

Jesus lived in perfect obedience to the Mosaic Law, fulfilling its requirements (Matthew 5:17).

Jesus' Fulfillment of the Law

"Do not think that I came to destroy the Law or the Prophets. I did not come to destroy but to fulfill." (Matthew 5:17, NKJV)

1. **Fulfillment (Greek: *plēroō*, πληρόω; Strong's G4137)**
   - Meaning: To complete or bring to fullness.
   - Jesus fulfilled the Law by perfectly embodying its moral and ethical standards and by being the ultimate sacrifice for sin (Hebrews 10:1-10).
2. **Living Under the Law**
   - Jesus adhered to Jewish traditions and laws, participating in festivals (John 2:13) and observing Sabbath regulations (Luke 4:16).
   - His obedience to the Law demonstrated His role as the spotless Lamb of God (1 Peter 1:19).

The New Covenant: A Paradigm Shift

From the Old to the New

Jesus' teachings and actions prepared the way for a new covenant that would transcend the Mosaic Law.

1. **The Promise of a New Covenant**
   - Prophesied by Jeremiah:

     "Behold, the days are coming, says the Lord, when I will make a new covenant with the house of Israel and with the house of Judah." (Jeremiah 31:31, NKJV)

   - Fulfilled in Christ's sacrificial death:

     "This cup is the new covenant in My blood, which is shed for you." (Luke 22:20, NKJV).

2. **Key Distinctions**
   - **Law of Moses**: External regulations written on stone (Exodus 34:1).
   - **Law of Christ**: Internal transformation through the Holy Spirit (2 Corinthians 3:3).

Jesus' Teachings: A Transition in Focus

Jesus' ministry emphasized the heart of the Law rather than its outward observance.

1. **Sermon on the Mount (Matthew 5-7)**

- o Jesus reinterpreted the Law, shifting from external compliance to internal righteousness.

  "You have heard that it was said to those of old, 'You shall not commit adultery.' But I say to you that whoever looks at a woman to lust for her has already committed adultery with her in his heart." (Matthew 5:27-28).

2. **The Greatest Commandments**
   - o Jesus summarized the Law in two principles:

     "You shall love the Lord your God with all your heart, with all your soul, and with all your mind. This is the first and great commandment. And the second is like it: You shall love your neighbor as yourself." (Matthew 22:37-39, NKJV).

   - o **Love (Greek: *agapē*, ἀγάπη; Strong's G26)** became the cornerstone of the new covenant.

The Law of Christ

Definition

The "Law of Christ" refers to the principles and commands established by Jesus and carried forward by His apostles.

1. **Galatians 6:2**

"Bear one another's burdens, and so fulfill the law of Christ."

- o **Bear (Greek: *bastazō*, βαστάζω; Strong's G941):** To carry or endure.
- o The Law of Christ emphasizes mutual love and support, reflecting Christ's sacrificial love.

2. **Romans 8:2**

"For the law of the Spirit of life in Christ Jesus has made me free from the law of sin and death."

- o The new covenant liberates believers from the penalty and power of sin, enabling them to live by the Spirit.

Strong's Concordance: Key Word Study

1. **Law (Greek: *nomos*, νόμος; Strong's G3551)**
   - o Refers to both the Mosaic Law and the broader principles of divine instruction.
   - o The Law of Christ represents a higher standard of love and grace.
2. **Covenant (Greek: *diathēkē*, διαθήκη; Strong's G1242)**
   - o A binding agreement.
   - o The new covenant is eternal, written on the hearts of believers (Hebrews 8:10).
3. **Fulfill (Greek: *plēroō*, πληρόω; Strong's G4137)**
   - o To bring to completion.
   - o Jesus fulfilled the Law by perfectly obeying it and inaugurating a new way of righteousness.

Expository Commentary

1. **Jesus as the Bridge**
   - Jesus did not abolish the Mosaic Law but fulfilled its purpose, revealing its ultimate intent: reconciliation with God through grace.
2. **The New Covenant's Inclusivity**
   - The Law of Christ extends beyond Israel to all humanity, emphasizing faith over works (Galatians 3:28).
3. **Practical Implications**
   - Believers are called to emulate Christ's love and selflessness, living by the Spirit rather than the letter of the Law (2 Corinthians 3:6).

Conclusion

Jesus' ministry under the Mosaic Law was foundational in transitioning to the Law of Christ. By fulfilling the Law's requirements and establishing a new covenant, Jesus redefined righteousness as an inward transformation driven by love and empowered by the Spirit. This paradigm shift invites believers to live in the freedom and fullness of Christ, guided by His example and teachings.

Through this transition, the story of redemption becomes accessible to all, emphasizing grace, faith, and the transformative power of God's love.

CHAPTER 04

PAUL'S TEACHING ON HOMOSEXUALITY

Explicit Condemnations of Homosexuality in Paul's Epistles

Paul's epistles in the New Testament contain some of the most explicit references to homosexuality. Through his writings, Paul addresses issues of sexual morality in the context of both Jewish law and the Greco-Roman culture of his time. This chapter examines the relevant passages, using Strong's Concordance for a detailed word study and offering a comprehensive commentary to understand Paul's theological and moral framework.

---

1. Romans 1:24-27

Textual Context

Paul's letter to the Romans begins with an indictment of humanity's rebellion against God. In this section, Paul highlights the consequences of idolatry, including moral and sexual degradation.

"Therefore God also gave them up to uncleanness, in the lusts of their hearts, to dishonor their bodies among themselves, who exchanged the truth of God for the lie, and worshiped and served the creature rather than the Creator... For this reason, God gave them up to vile passions. For even their women exchanged the natural use for what is against nature. Likewise also the men, leaving the natural use of the woman, burned in their lust for one another, men with men committing what is shameful, and receiving in themselves the penalty of their error which was due." (Romans 1:24-27, NKJV)

Key Terms and Analysis

1. **Uncleanness (Greek: *akatharsia*, ἀκαθαρσία; Strong's G167)**
     - Refers to moral impurity, especially sexual immorality.
     - Paul ties this term to idolatry, suggesting that rejecting God leads to corrupt desires.

2. **Vile Passions (Greek: *pathē atimias*, πάθη ἀτιμίας; Strong's G3806 & G819)**
   o **Pathē**: Inordinate affections or strong desires.
   o **Atimias**: Dishonor or disgrace.
   o These terms highlight the degrading nature of sexual sins that deviate from God's design.
3. **Against Nature (Greek: *para physin*, παρὰ φύσιν; Strong's G5449)**
   o Literally, "contrary to natural order."
   o Paul emphasizes that same-sex relations violate the intended biological and moral purposes of human sexuality.
4. **Shameful (Greek: *aschēmosynē*, ἀσχημοσύνη; Strong's G808)**
   o A term denoting indecency or moral offensiveness.
   o Paul characterizes homosexual acts as inherently dishonorable.

Theological Commentary

- **Divine Judgment**: Paul views homosexual behavior as both a consequence and a symptom of humanity's rejection of God.
- **Natural Order**: The phrase "against nature" reflects the creation narrative in Genesis, where sexual union is designed for male and female partnership.
- **Cultural Relevance**: Paul's condemnation speaks against practices common in the Greco-Roman world, such as pederasty and temple prostitution.

---

2. 1 Corinthians 6:9-11

Textual Context

In this passage, Paul warns the Corinthians against unrighteous behavior that excludes individuals from God's kingdom.

"Do you not know that the unrighteous will not inherit the kingdom of God? Do not be deceived. Neither fornicators, nor idolaters, nor adulterers, nor homosexuals, nor sodomites, nor thieves, nor covetous, nor drunkards, nor revilers, nor extortioners will inherit the kingdom of God. And such were some of you. But you were washed, but you were sanctified, but you were justified in the name of the Lord Jesus and by the Spirit of our God." (1 Corinthians 6:9-11, NKJV)

Key Terms and Analysis

1. **Homosexuals (Greek: *malakoi*, μαλακοί; Strong's G3120)**
   - Literally "soft" or "effeminate."
   - Often interpreted as referring to the passive partner in homosexual acts.
2. **Sodomites (Greek: *arsenokoitai*, ἀρσενοκοῖται; Strong's G733)**
   - Compound of *arsen* (male) and *koitē* (bed).
   - Denotes those who engage in same-sex relations.
3. **Sanctified (Greek: *hagiazo*, ἁγιάζω; Strong's G37)**
   - Refers to being set apart for God's purposes.
   - Paul highlights the transformative power of God's grace in delivering believers from sinful behaviors.

Theological Commentary

- **Kingdom Ethics**: Paul categorizes homosexual acts alongside other sins that disqualify individuals from inheriting God's kingdom.
- **Grace and Redemption**: Paul's message offers hope, emphasizing that past sins can be forgiven through repentance and faith.
- **Cultural Specificity**: The terms *malakoi* and *arsenokoitai* address specific practices in Greco-Roman society while affirming universal moral principles.

3. 1 Timothy 1:9-10

Textual Context

Paul, writing to Timothy, lists various sins to illustrate the purpose of the law in restraining ungodliness.

"...the law is not made for a righteous person, but for the lawless and insubordinate, for the ungodly and for sinners, for the unholy and profane, for murderers of fathers and murderers of mothers, for manslayers, for fornicators, for sodomites, for kidnappers, for liars, for perjurers, and if there is any other thing that is contrary to sound doctrine." (1 Timothy 1:9-10, NKJV)

Key Terms and Analysis

1. **Sodomites (*arsenokoitai*, ἀρσενοκοῖται; Strong's G733)**
   - As in 1 Corinthians 6:9, this term refers to male same-sex relations.

2. **Sound Doctrine (Greek: *hygiainousa didaskalia*, ὑγιαίνουσα διδασκαλία; Strong's G5198 & G1319)**
   o "Healthy teaching" aligned with God's moral order.
   o Paul connects sexual sins with a broader rejection of divine truth.

Theological Commentary

- **Purpose of the Law**: Paul underscores that the law serves to expose sin and highlight humanity's need for a Savior.
- **Sound Doctrine**: Sexual ethics are rooted in God's design and integral to Christian teaching.
- **Pastoral Concern**: Paul's warnings aim to guide believers toward holiness and away from cultural influences that compromise moral integrity.

Conclusion

Paul's teachings on homosexuality are clear and rooted in a broader framework of biblical sexual ethics. By addressing same-sex behavior within the context of idolatry, natural law, and kingdom values, Paul emphasizes the incompatibility of such acts with God's design.

Key takeaways include:

1. The importance of aligning sexual behavior with God's created order.
2. The role of grace in redeeming individuals from sin.
3. The continued relevance of biblical morality in addressing contemporary issues.

Through careful exegesis and word study, this chapter demonstrates that Paul's condemnation of homosexuality is consistent with the overarching message of Scripture: God's holiness demands moral purity, but His grace offers redemption and transformation for all who repent and believe.

The Broader Term of Fornication

Understanding Fornication in the New Testament

The term *fornication* (Greek: **porneia**, πορνεία; Strong's G4202) encompasses a broad range of sexual sins, including but not limited to adultery, incest, prostitution, and homosexual acts. The New Testament writers, under the inspiration of the Holy Spirit, used the term to maintain continuity with the moral laws outlined in the Old Testament while emphasizing the new covenant's transformative power. This chapter explores how homosexual acts, along with other forms of sexual immorality, fall under the broader category of *fornication.*

1. Porneia in the Teachings of Jesus

In passages such as Matthew 15:19, Jesus lists *fornication* as one of the sins that defile a person:

"For out of the heart proceed evil thoughts, murders, adulteries, fornications (porneiai), thefts, false witness, blasphemies." (Matthew 15:19, NKJV)

Key Terms and Analysis

- **Fornications (*porneiai*, πορνεῖαι; plural of *porneia*)**
  - Refers broadly to all sexual practices outside the sanctity of marriage.
  - Jesus underscores the internal origin of such sins, linking them to the heart's sinful desires.
- **Defilement (Greek: *koinoo*, κοινόω; Strong's G2840)**
  - Indicates a spiritual impurity that separates individuals from God.

Theological Commentary

Jesus' mention of *fornication* encompasses a range of sexual behaviors, aligning with the Mosaic Law's prohibitions (Leviticus 18). By addressing the root—sinful desires—Jesus expands the concept of sexual immorality beyond external actions to include internal dispositions, thereby setting the stage for New Testament teachings on purity and holiness.

2. Porneia in Paul's Writings

1 Corinthians 6:18-20

Paul exhorts believers to flee *fornication*, emphasizing its unique effect on the body:

"Flee sexual immorality (porneia). Every sin that a man does is outside the body, but he who commits sexual immorality sins against his own body. Or do you not know that your body is the temple of the Holy Spirit who is in you, whom you have

from God, and you are not your own?" (1 Corinthians 6:18-19, NKJV)

Key Terms and Analysis

1. **Sexual Immorality (*porneia*)**
    o   Includes all sexual acts outside of God's design for marriage.
    o   Homosexual acts are inherently included as deviations from the creation ordinance (Genesis 2:24).
2. **Temple (Greek: *naos*, ναός; Strong's G3485)**
    o   Refers to the believer's body as a dwelling place of the Holy Spirit.
    o   Sexual sins defile this sacred dwelling, violating both the physical body and spiritual identity.

Theological Commentary

*   Paul broadens the definition of *porneia* to address all forms of sexual immorality within the Christian community.
*   His teachings stress the sanctity of the body as God's temple, making any sexual deviation, including homosexuality, incompatible with a life dedicated to holiness.

---

3. Jude 1:7 – Sodom and Fornication

Jude draws a parallel between the sexual immorality of Sodom and Gomorrah and the broader term *fornication*:

"As Sodom and Gomorrah, and the cities around them in a similar manner to these, having given themselves over to sexual immorality (ekporneuo) and gone after strange flesh, are set forth as an example, suffering the vengeance of eternal fire." (Jude 1:7, NKJV)

Key Terms and Analysis

1. **Sexual Immorality (*ekporneuo*, ἐκπορνεύω; Strong's G1608)**
   o Intensified form of *porneia*, indicating extreme or unrestrained immorality.
2. **Strange Flesh (Greek: *sarkos heteras*, σαρκὸς ἑτέρας; Strong's G4561 & G2087)**
   o Refers to unnatural sexual relations, often interpreted as same-sex acts or relations with non-human entities.

Theological Commentary

Jude's condemnation of Sodom connects homosexual behavior to *porneia*, illustrating the ongoing relevance of this term in the New Testament's moral framework. The passage underscores divine judgment against sexual immorality as a universal principle.

4. Revelation 22:15 – Fornicators Excluded

In the closing verses of Revelation, John lists *fornicators* among those excluded from the New Jerusalem:

"But outside are dogs and sorcerers and sexually immoral (pornos), and murderers and idolaters, and whoever loves and practices a lie." (Revelation 22:15, NKJV)

Key Terms and Analysis

1. **Sexually Immoral (*pornos*, πόρνος; Strong's G4205)**
   - A term derived from *porneia*, encompassing individuals who engage in illicit sexual acts.
2. **Outside (Greek: *exō*, ἔξω; Strong's G1854)**
   - Refers to exclusion from God's eternal presence and blessings.

Theological Commentary

- John's vision confirms the eternal consequences of unrepentant sexual immorality.
- The inclusion of *pornos* highlights the consistency of biblical teachings on sexual ethics from Genesis to Revelation.

Conclusion

The New Testament consistently categorizes homosexual acts within the broader term *fornication*, maintaining continuity with the Mosaic Law while expanding the understanding of sexual immorality under the new covenant. The writers, inspired by the Holy Spirit, present *porneia* as a violation of

God's design for human relationships, offering both warnings of judgment and the hope of redemption through Christ.

Authority and Inspiration of Scripture

Understanding the Inspiration of Scripture

The doctrine of the inspiration of Scripture serves as the foundation for understanding its authority and reliability. The apostle Paul declares:

"All Scripture is given by inspiration of God, and is profitable for doctrine, for reproof, for correction, for instruction in righteousness, that the man of God may be complete, thoroughly equipped for every good work." (2 Timothy 3:16-17, NKJV)

This statement highlights the divine origin of Scripture, its comprehensive authority, and its application to Christian life and doctrine. By extension, the apostolic teachings—including those addressing sexual morality—carry the authority of Christ Himself, as they are rooted in divine inspiration.

1. The Meaning of Inspiration

The term *inspiration* is translated from the Greek word **theopneustos** (θεόπνευστος; Strong's G2315), meaning "God-breathed." This word underscores the divine source of Scripture, indicating that God is the ultimate author, working through human writers to convey His will without error.

- **Theopneustos**: A unique term in the New Testament, emphasizing that Scripture originates from the breath of God, much like the breath of life given to humanity in creation (Genesis 2:7).

Theological Significance

1. **Unity of Scripture**: All Scripture, from Genesis to Revelation, is unified in its purpose and divine origin, making the New Testament teachings inseparable from the authority of Christ.
2. **Apostolic Authority**: The writings of Paul, Peter, John, and other apostles are divinely inspired, ensuring that their teachings align with the will and character of God.

---

2. Christ's Affirmation of Scripture

Jesus frequently affirmed the authority of Scripture during His earthly ministry, referencing the Old Testament as the Word of God:

"Your word is truth." (John 17:17, NKJV)

"For assuredly, I say to you, till heaven and earth pass away, one jot or one tittle will by no means pass from the law till all is fulfilled." (Matthew 5:18, NKJV)

Jesus' use of Scripture to counter temptation (Matthew 4:4-10) and His assertion that it cannot be broken (John 10:35) further confirm its divine authority.

---

3. Apostolic Teachings and the Authority of Christ

The apostles consistently claimed that their teachings were not merely human opinions but divinely inspired truths rooted in the authority of Christ.

- **Paul's Declaration**:

  "For I delivered to you first of all that which I also received: that Christ died for our sins according to the Scriptures." (1 Corinthians 15:3, NKJV)

  This statement demonstrates Paul's reliance on both Old Testament prophecy and divine revelation.

- **Peter's Affirmation**:

  "Knowing this first, that no prophecy of Scripture is of any private interpretation, for prophecy never came by the will of man, but holy men of God spoke as they were moved by the Holy Spirit." (2 Peter 1:20-21, NKJV)

  Peter highlights the Spirit's role in guiding the writing of Scripture, affirming its reliability and divine origin.

---

4. The New Testament and Sexual Morality

The authority of Scripture extends to its moral teachings, including those concerning sexuality. Paul's epistles, inspired by the Holy Spirit, explicitly address issues like fornication, adultery, and homosexuality:

- **Romans 1:24-27**: Paul describes the consequences of humanity's rejection of God, including dishonorable

passions and homosexual acts, as evidence of spiritual rebellion.
- **1 Corinthians 6:9-10**: Paul lists those who will not inherit the kingdom of God, including *arsenokoitai* (those who practice homosexuality), categorizing such acts as incompatible with a life devoted to Christ.
- **1 Timothy 1:9-10**: Paul reiterates the inclusion of homosexual acts among sins contrary to sound doctrine.

By affirming the divine inspiration of these writings, the New Testament demonstrates that its moral teachings are authoritative and binding for all believers.

5. Practical Implications of Scriptural Authority

1. **Doctrine and Reproof** Scripture provides a reliable standard for teaching and correcting moral behavior. For example, the apostolic condemnation of homosexual acts is not arbitrary but grounded in God's consistent moral order.
2. **Correction and Instruction** Scripture equips believers to pursue righteousness, offering both the diagnosis of sin and the hope of redemption through Christ.
3. **Equipping for Good Works** As Paul states in 2 Timothy 3:17, Scripture prepares believers to live holy lives, reflecting God's character in all aspects of life, including their approach to sexual ethics.

6. Conclusion: Scripture as the Foundation of Authority

The authority and inspiration of Scripture, as articulated in 2 Timothy 3:16-17, affirm that all biblical teachings, including those on sexual morality, represent the will of God. Jesus' affirmation of Scripture and the apostles' inspired writings further underscore its reliability and relevance. For believers, adherence to the teachings of Scripture is not optional but a fundamental aspect of discipleship, reflecting submission to the authority of Christ.

In recognizing the divine inspiration of Scripture, we are reminded of its role as a guiding light:

"Your word is a lamp to my feet and a light to my path." (Psalm 119:105, NKJV)

Thus, the moral teachings found within, including those addressing fornication and homosexuality, are to be understood as timeless truths rooted in the character and authority of God Himself.

CHAPTER 05

JESUS AND THE JUDGMENT OF SODOM

The Judgment of Sodom

The story of Sodom and Gomorrah serves as a powerful biblical narrative symbolizing divine judgment against sin, particularly sexual immorality and injustice. This account, found in Genesis 18-19, has been referenced by both Jewish and Christian traditions to illustrate God's justice and mercy. Jesus Himself referred to Sodom's judgment as a warning against unrepentance and a lack of faith, linking it to the ultimate day of judgment.

In this chapter, we explore the judgment of Sodom, the historical and theological significance of its location, and its relevance in the teachings of Jesus.

---

1. What Is the Judgment of Sodom?

The judgment of Sodom and Gomorrah is described in Genesis 19:24-25:

"Then the Lord rained brimstone and fire on Sodom and Gomorrah, from the Lord out of the heavens. So He overthrew those cities, all the plain, all the inhabitants of the cities, and what grew on the ground."

The narrative identifies specific sins, such as pride, oppression, and sexual immorality, as the cause of their destruction (Ezekiel 16:49-50; Jude 1:7). Among these, the attempt by the men of Sodom to commit acts of sexual violence (Genesis 19:4-5) is presented as a manifestation of their depravity.

- **Judgment by Fire**: Fire and brimstone symbolize God's righteous wrath and His power to purify and cleanse.
- **Total Destruction**: The annihilation of Sodom and Gomorrah serves as a warning of the severity of divine judgment for unrepentant sin.

---

2. Where Were Sodom and Gomorrah?

The exact location of Sodom and Gomorrah has been a subject of archaeological and historical inquiry. The cities were part of the "Cities of the Plain" near the Dead Sea region.

- **Possible Locations**: Archaeological sites such as Bab edh-Dhra and Numeira have been proposed as candidates for the ruins of Sodom and Gomorrah. These sites exhibit evidence of sudden destruction by fire, consistent with the biblical account.
- **Geographical Context**:
  - The Dead Sea region is known for its high sulfur content and geological instability, supporting the narrative of brimstone and fire.
  - The area was once fertile, described as being "like the garden of the Lord" (Genesis 13:10), but is now barren, a testament to the aftermath of divine judgment.

---

3. Sodom and Gomorrah in the Teachings of Jesus

Jesus referenced Sodom and Gomorrah multiple times to warn of the consequences of rejecting God's message:

- **Judgment for Unrepentance**:

  "And whoever will not receive you nor hear your words, when you depart from that house or city, shake off the dust from your feet. Assuredly, I say to you, it will be more tolerable for the land of Sodom and Gomorrah in the day of judgment than for that city!" (Matthew 10:14-15, NKJV)

  Jesus used Sodom's judgment as a comparison to emphasize the accountability of those who hear and reject the gospel.

- **Significance in Luke 17:28-30**:

"Likewise as it was also in the days of Lot: They ate, they drank, they bought, they sold, they planted, they built; but on the day that Lot went out of Sodom it rained fire and brimstone from heaven and destroyed them all. Even so will it be in the day when the Son of Man is revealed."

Jesus draws a parallel between the complacency of Sodom's inhabitants and the apathy that will precede His return, underscoring the need for vigilance and repentance.

---

4. Lessons from Sodom and Gomorrah

1. **God's Justice**: The destruction of Sodom and Gomorrah illustrates God's intolerance of sin and His commitment to justice. As Ezekiel 16:49-50 notes, their sins included pride, neglect of the poor, and abominable acts, showing the breadth of their rebellion against God.
2. **God's Mercy**: Despite their wickedness, God's willingness to spare the cities if ten righteous people were found (Genesis 18:32) demonstrates His mercy. Lot's rescue further highlights God's grace toward the righteous.
3. **A Warning for All Generations**: The apostle Jude identifies Sodom's destruction as a warning:

"As Sodom and Gomorrah, and the cities around them in a similar manner to these, having given themselves over to sexual immorality and gone after strange flesh,

are set forth as an example, suffering the vengeance of eternal fire. " (Jude 1:7, NKJV)

This warning emphasizes the eternal consequences of unrepentant sin.

---

5. Contemporary Relevance

The story of Sodom and Gomorrah remains relevant for understanding divine judgment and the call to holiness:

- **Sexual Morality**: The narrative underscores the seriousness of sexual sin and its consequences, calling believers to align with biblical principles.
- **Social Justice**: Ezekiel 16:49 reminds us that pride and neglect of the needy were also sins of Sodom, highlighting the need for compassion and justice.
- **Call to Repentance**: Like Sodom, modern societies are accountable for their response to God's truth. Jesus' warnings challenge us to embrace repentance and faith.

---

6. Conclusion: The Judgment of Sodom and the Gospel

The judgment of Sodom and Gomorrah is a profound testament to God's justice, mercy, and holiness. As Jesus warned, the fate of Sodom serves as a shadow of the ultimate judgment awaiting those who reject the gospel. However, the story also reveals God's desire to save the righteous and His patience in offering opportunities for repentance.

The destruction of Sodom challenges believers to reflect on their own lives, communities, and response to God's call:

"The Lord is not slack concerning His promise, as some count slackness, but is longsuffering toward us, not willing that any should perish but that all should come to repentance." (2 Peter 3:9, NKJV)

Through Christ, we are offered redemption and the hope of avoiding judgment—a powerful reminder of God's grace in the face of human sin.

Jesus' Reference to Sodom

Introduction: Jesus and the Days of Sodom

Jesus frequently referenced historical events to illustrate profound spiritual truths, and His mention of Sodom holds significant theological implications. In Luke 17:29-30, Jesus compares His second coming to the days of Sodom, emphasizing the suddenness of divine judgment and humanity's tendency toward complacency.

This chapter explores Jesus' reference to Sodom in the context of His teachings, its eschatological significance, and its broader implications for understanding the judgment of sin.

1. Context of Luke 17:29-30

The passage reads:

"But on the day that Lot went out of Sodom it rained fire and brimstone from heaven and destroyed them all. Even so will it be in the day when the Son of Man is revealed." (Luke 17:29-30, NKJV)

In this discourse, Jesus warns His disciples about the unexpected nature of His return, drawing parallels between the attitudes of the people in Sodom and those living in the last days.

- **Setting the Scene**: Jesus speaks to His disciples about the kingdom of God and the signs of His return (Luke 17:20-37). His reference to Sodom serves as a vivid reminder of the judgment that accompanies God's intervention in history.
- **Sodom's Historical Judgment**: The story of Sodom's destruction in Genesis 19 illustrates God's justice against rampant sin and the rescue of the righteous, typified by Lot and his family.

---

2. The Days of Sodom: A Snapshot of Human Sin

The "days of Sodom" symbolize a society consumed by moral decay and spiritual blindness. Genesis 19:4-5 reveals the depravity of Sodom's inhabitants, whose sins included:

- **Sexual Immorality**: The men of Sodom sought to commit egregious acts of sexual violence, symbolizing their rejection of divine order (Jude 1:7).
- **Pride and Injustice**: Ezekiel 16:49-50 identifies their arrogance, neglect of the poor, and detestable practices as contributing to their judgment.

The complacency and self-indulgence of Sodom reflect the attitudes Jesus warns against in Luke 17.

3. Theological Implications of Jesus' Comparison

1. **Suddenness of Judgment**: Jesus emphasizes that, like the destruction of Sodom, His return will be sudden and unexpected. People will be going about their daily lives—eating, drinking, buying, selling, planting, and building—when judgment arrives (Luke 17:28).
    - The imagery underscores the danger of spiritual complacency.
    - It serves as a call to vigilance and readiness for Christ's return.
2. **The Universality of Judgment**: Just as Sodom's judgment was total and inescapable, so too will the judgment at Jesus' second coming be comprehensive. Revelation 6:16-17 reiterates that no one can stand before the wrath of the Lamb without faith and repentance.
3. **Rescue of the Righteous**: The deliverance of Lot highlights God's mercy toward the faithful. In the same way, Jesus promises salvation to those who trust in Him, even as the world faces judgment (2 Peter 2:7-9).

4. Eschatological Significance of Sodom's Judgment

Jesus' reference to Sodom aligns with other eschatological teachings about the Day of the Lord:

- **Signs of the Times**: The moral and spiritual conditions of the days of Sodom mirror the conditions preceding Christ's return. 2 Timothy 3:1-5 describes these days as marked by selfishness, arrogance, and godlessness.

- **A Forewarning of Eternal Judgment**: Sodom's destruction by fire and brimstone serves as a precursor to the ultimate judgment, described as the "lake of fire" in Revelation 20:15. Jude 1:7 calls Sodom an example of eternal punishment for unrepentant sin.

5. Jesus' Call to Readiness

In Luke 17:32, Jesus says:

"Remember Lot's wife."

This brief yet powerful statement warns against divided loyalties and the dangers of clinging to worldly attachments. Lot's wife, who looked back at Sodom, symbolizes those who hesitate to fully embrace God's call to righteousness (Genesis 19:26).

- **Application for Believers**:
    - Avoid the temptation to prioritize earthly pursuits over spiritual readiness.
    - Trust in God's provision and guidance, even when it requires leaving behind comfort and familiarity.

6. Practical Lessons from Jesus' Reference to Sodom

1. **The Urgency of Repentance**: Jesus' comparison underscores the necessity of turning from sin and

seeking His forgiveness before it is too late. As 2 Peter 3:9 reminds us:

"The Lord is not slack concerning His promise, as some count slackness, but is longsuffering toward us, not willing that any should perish but that all should come to repentance."

2. **The Call to Holy Living**: Believers are called to stand apart from a culture of immorality and to live as witnesses to God's truth.
3. **Faith in God's Justice and Mercy**: Sodom's destruction reveals God's justice, but Lot's rescue demonstrates His mercy toward the faithful. This dual aspect of God's character offers both a warning and a promise.

---

7. Conclusion: Sodom as a Warning and Hope

Jesus' reference to Sodom in Luke 17:29-30 serves as both a cautionary tale and a reminder of God's ultimate plan for humanity. It highlights the reality of judgment, the urgency of repentance, and the hope of salvation through Christ.

As we reflect on the days of Sodom, let us heed Jesus' warning and strive to live in readiness for His return. For those who trust in Him, the day of judgment is not a day of fear, but a day of deliverance and eternal reward:

"For God did not appoint us to wrath, but to obtain salvation through our Lord Jesus Christ." (1 Thessalonians 5:9, NKJV)

Sodom as an Example in Jude

Introduction: Jude's Warning Against "Strange Flesh"

The Book of Jude is a short but powerful epistle located near the end of the New Testament. It addresses various issues concerning false teachers, immorality, and the consequences of turning away from God's truth. In Jude 7, the author references the infamous destruction of Sodom and Gomorrah, particularly noting the sin that led to their demise. This passage, which mentions people "going after strange flesh," is widely interpreted as a divine condemnation of homosexual acts. This chapter will explore the context of Jude 7, its meaning, and how it links the judgment of Sodom to the broader biblical teachings on sexual morality.

1. The Context of Jude's Epistle

Jude identifies himself as the brother of James (Jude 1:1) and writes primarily to Christians who are facing the influence of false teachers and immoral practices. The letter's themes of judgment, holiness, and the necessity of guarding the faith are evident throughout. Jude is concerned about individuals who have "crept in unnoticed" and who "turn the grace of our God into lewdness" (Jude 1:4). The sinfulness of Sodom and Gomorrah serves as a prime example of what awaits those who reject God's moral order.

Jude's mention of Sodom and Gomorrah is tied to the larger theme of God's judgment against immorality and perversion. By warning his audience to avoid the same fate, Jude underscores the dire consequences of departing from divine standards of holiness.

---

2. *Understanding Jude 7: "Going After Strange Flesh"*

Jude 7 states:

"As Sodom and Gomorrah, and the cities around them in similar manner to these, having given themselves over to sexual immorality and gone after strange flesh, are set forth as an example, suffering the vengeance of eternal fire." (Jude 1:7, NKJV)

Key terms in this verse—"strange flesh" and "sexual immorality"—are crucial for interpreting the nature of the sin for which Sodom and Gomorrah were condemned.

- **"Strange Flesh"**: The phrase "strange flesh" has been understood by many scholars and theologians to refer to unnatural or forbidden sexual relations, often interpreted as homosexual acts. The Greek word *"heteros"* (meaning "other" or "different") is used in various contexts in the New Testament, implying relations that go beyond the natural order established by God. In the case of Sodom, this "strange flesh" was understood as same-sex sexual activity, specifically the violent and aggressive sexual behavior exhibited by the men of Sodom toward Lot's guests (Genesis 19:4-5).
- **Sexual Immorality**: The term *porneia* is commonly used in the New Testament to describe all forms of illicit sexual behavior, including adultery, fornication,

and homosexual acts. In this case, it refers to the overall sexual depravity and perversion that characterized Sodom and Gomorrah, culminating in the desire for "strange flesh." Jude uses this term to emphasize that the cities of Sodom and Gomorrah were engaged in practices that were explicitly forbidden by God's moral law.

3. The Sodom and Gomorrah Narrative in Genesis 19

To understand the reference in Jude, it is important to revisit the biblical account of Sodom and Gomorrah in Genesis 19. The key event leading to the destruction of the two cities involves the attempted homosexual assault on Lot's angelic guests. The men of Sodom surround Lot's house and demand that he send out the visitors so they can "know" (a biblical euphemism for sexual intercourse) them (Genesis 19:4-5). Lot, in a desperate attempt to protect his guests, offers his daughters instead, but the crowd rejects this offer, displaying the depth of their moral corruption.

- **Divine Condemnation**: In response to the wickedness of the Sodomites, God sends two angels to warn Lot and his family to flee. The cities are then destroyed by fire and brimstone as a divine judgment for their sin (Genesis 19:24-25). This destruction serves as a clear example of God's severe judgment on sexual immorality and other forms of wickedness.
- **Homosexual Sin**: The sin of Sodom, widely interpreted as homosexual behavior, is not the sole reason for their destruction, but it is a central component. Ezekiel 16:49-50 provides a broader explanation for Sodom's sinfulness, highlighting pride, oppression of the poor, and general wickedness.

However, the attempted homosexual acts in Genesis 19 provide a stark representation of the abomination that God found in their practices.

4. The Use of Sodom as an Example

Jude 7 explicitly states that the fate of Sodom and Gomorrah serves as an example for those who follow in their sinful ways. The destruction of these cities is a warning of "eternal fire," a symbol of the final judgment. This serves as a reminder that those who engage in practices that defy God's created order will face judgment, just as Sodom and Gomorrah did.

The reference to Sodom is not isolated. Jesus Himself references the judgment of Sodom in the Gospels, particularly in Matthew 10:15 and Luke 10:12, as a warning to those who reject the gospel. The cities of the plain, known for their immorality, are depicted as epitomizing the consequences of rejecting God's laws and embracing perversion.

5. The Broader Biblical View of Homosexuality

Jude 7's reference to "strange flesh" aligns with other parts of Scripture that condemn homosexual behavior:

- **Leviticus 18:22 and 20:13**: These passages in the Old Testament law explicitly forbid male-male sexual relations, calling them an abomination. The prohibition is part of a broader moral code that upholds the sanctity of marriage and sexual purity.
- **Romans 1:26-27**: Paul's letter to the Romans describes how people "exchanged the natural use of the woman for

what is against nature," referring to homosexual acts as a result of humanity's rejection of God.

- **1 Corinthians 6:9-10**: Paul lists those who will not inherit the kingdom of God, including "the sexually immoral" and "men who have sex with men" (NIV).

These passages reinforce the understanding that homosexual acts, as described in both the Old and New Testaments, are sinful in the eyes of God and stand as a violation of His created order.

---

6. Theological Implications of Jude's Warning

The reference to Sodom in Jude 7 is a significant theological statement about the nature of sin, divine justice, and the need for repentance. It teaches several key lessons:

- **The Wrath of God Against Sin**: Jude's epistle, like the story of Sodom, emphasizes that God will judge sin, especially sexual immorality, in its various forms. The wrath of God against Sodom is not simply a historical event but a warning for all people to turn from sin and seek God's forgiveness.
- **The Necessity of Holiness**: Just as Sodom was destroyed because of its unrepentant sin, believers are called to live holy lives that reflect God's will. The call to holiness is central to the Christian life, and the example of Sodom serves as a stark reminder of the consequences of ignoring God's moral standards.
- **The Hope of Salvation**: While the destruction of Sodom serves as a warning, it also serves as a reminder that God's mercy is available to those who repent. Lot's escape from the city, though flawed in many

ways, shows that God delivers the righteous from judgment.

---

7. Conclusion: Sodom as a Warning for Today

Jude 7 powerfully links the judgment of Sodom with the rejection of divine morality, particularly in the area of sexual ethics. By referring to the cities as examples of those who "go after strange flesh," Jude condemns the same sinful practices that led to their downfall. The epistle stands as a clear warning to all people that living in defiance of God's commandments brings judgment, but also that repentance and faith in Christ offer a way of salvation. The example of Sodom is timeless, reminding both Christians and non-believers of the need for repentance and adherence to God's standards for living.

Jesus' Loving Yet Righteous Judgment

Introduction: The Tension Between Love and Judgment

The life and teachings of Jesus present a unique and often misunderstood tension between His love for humanity and His call to repentance and obedience. Jesus is portrayed throughout the Gospels as a compassionate, loving Savior who welcomed sinners, healed the sick, and sought out the marginalized. However, alongside His boundless love, Jesus also called people to repentance, warning of the consequences of sin and declaring that transformation and obedience to God were essential for salvation. This chapter explores the delicate balance between Jesus' loving nature and His righteous judgment, emphasizing that love does not mean the absence of accountability and transformation.

---

1. Jesus' Love for All People

At the core of Jesus' ministry was His love for all people, regardless of their social status, past sins, or personal failures. Throughout His life, He reached out to those whom society often rejected—tax collectors, sinners, and outcasts—and extended His grace and mercy to them.

- **Matthew 11:28-30**: Jesus invites all who are weary and burdened to come to Him for rest, saying, *"Come to me, all you who are weary and burdened, and I will give you rest. Take my yoke upon you and learn from me, for I am gentle and humble in heart, and you will find rest for your souls."* This invitation reflects Jesus' love for all, offering peace and rest to those who feel overwhelmed by their sin and struggles.
- **Luke 19:10**: Jesus states His mission clearly: *"For the Son of Man came to seek and to save the lost."* This shows that Jesus' love was not just for the righteous, but for those who were lost and separated from God.
- **John 3:16**: The most famous verse in the New Testament encapsulates the scope of Jesus' love: *"For God so loved the world that he gave his one and only Son, that whoever believes in him shall not perish but have eternal life."* This verse highlights the universal nature of God's love, as Jesus came to save the world, offering eternal life to anyone who believes in Him.

Jesus demonstrated that His love was not limited to a specific group of people; He loved even His enemies and those who did not deserve His love. His approach to sinners was always one of grace, offering forgiveness and healing.

---

2. Jesus' Call to Repentance

While Jesus loved everyone, He did not condone sin. His ministry was marked by a repeated call to repentance, urging people to turn away from their sins and live according to God's will. Jesus made it clear that while God's love is available to all, repentance and transformation are required for salvation.

- **Matthew 4:17**: At the beginning of His ministry, Jesus preached: *"Repent, for the kingdom of heaven has come near."* This was a call to a radical change of heart and life. Repentance, which means to turn away from sin and turn toward God, was the first step in entering the kingdom of heaven.
- **Luke 13:3**: Jesus warns, *"I tell you, no! But unless you repent, you too will all perish."* This verse emphasizes that repentance is not optional for those who seek salvation. Jesus warns that failure to repent leads to spiritual death.
- **Mark 1:15**: Jesus proclaims: *"The time has come. The kingdom of God has come near. Repent and believe the good news!"* This is a clear command to acknowledge one's sinful state and respond in faith to the gospel message.

Jesus' call to repentance was not merely an invitation; it was a command. Repentance was central to His message, signaling that while God's grace and love are available, they require a response from the individual. It was not enough to simply receive Jesus' love; people were called to change their lives in accordance with God's will.

---

3. Jesus' Righteous Judgment

Though Jesus is often associated with love, He was also the ultimate judge who would hold humanity accountable for their actions. His love did not diminish His authority to judge sin. Jesus consistently taught that there would be consequences for those who rejected Him and refused to repent.

- **Matthew 25:31-46**: In the parable of the sheep and the goats, Jesus depicts the final judgment where He will separate the righteous from the unrighteous. Those who have served others in love, representing their faith in Christ, will inherit the kingdom of God, while those who rejected His message will be condemned to eternal punishment. Jesus says, *"Then they will go away to eternal punishment, but the righteous to eternal life."* (Matthew 25:46)
- **John 5:22-23**: Jesus speaks of His role as judge: *"Moreover, the Father judges no one, but has entrusted all judgment to the Son, that all may honor the Son just as they honor the Father."* Jesus clearly states that He has the authority to judge all people, affirming His righteousness and the seriousness of His role in the final judgment.
- **Revelation 19:11-16**: Jesus is depicted as a righteous judge who will return in glory to judge the nations. *"With justice he judges and makes war."* This vision of Jesus as a righteous judge contrasts with the image of the loving Savior but underscores the truth that both love and judgment are essential aspects of His identity.

- **John 3:36**: Jesus clarifies that belief in Him leads to eternal life, but rejection of Him leads to judgment: *"Whoever believes in the Son has eternal life, but whoever rejects the Son will not see life, for God's wrath remains on them."* This warning reveals that while Jesus offers eternal life through faith, there is a real judgment for those who refuse His message.

---

4. Transformation and Obedience: The Path to Salvation

Jesus' loving yet righteous judgment is a call to both transformation and obedience. The invitation to salvation is extended to all, but it is a gift that must be received through faith and repentance. True discipleship involves not only believing in Jesus but also living in accordance with His teachings.

- **John 14:15**: Jesus emphasizes the connection between love for Him and obedience: *"If you love me, keep my commands."* This command to obey is not burdensome but flows from a relationship of love. True love for Jesus manifests in obedience to His will.
- **Luke 9:23**: Jesus calls His followers to self-denial and taking up their cross daily: *"Whoever wants to be my disciple must deny themselves and take up their cross daily and follow me."* This call to self-sacrifice highlights the transformative nature of following Jesus. It is not a passive love but an active commitment to live in accordance with His will.
- **Romans 12:1-2**: Paul, building on the teachings of Jesus, urges believers to present their bodies as living sacrifices, holy and pleasing to God. This call to

transform one's life through the renewing of the mind speaks to the radical change that Jesus expects from those who follow Him. *"Do not conform to the pattern of this world, but be transformed by the renewing of your mind."* (Romans 12:2)

Jesus' love calls people to transformation—heart, mind, and actions. Obedience to His commands is evidence of genuine repentance and faith. It is not enough to claim to love Jesus; true love for Him results in a life of obedience to His will.

5. Conclusion: The Balance of Love and Judgment

The life of Jesus reveals a profound balance between His love for humanity and His righteous judgment. While Jesus extended grace and mercy to all, offering forgiveness and eternal life, He also proclaimed the necessity of repentance and obedience. The invitation to salvation is open to all, but it requires a response—a transformation that comes through faith and repentance.

Jesus' love is unconditional, but His judgment is just. He calls people to repentance because He desires to save them, but He will not tolerate sin. The story of Jesus' ministry and the ultimate judgment at His second coming reflect the truth that salvation involves both love and transformation, and those who reject His call will face the consequences of their sin.

Thus, Jesus' loving yet righteous judgment is a call to both sinners and saints alike—to accept His love, repent of sin, and live in obedience to His will, knowing that His judgment is coming, but so is His grace.

CHAPTER 06

LOVE AND TOLERANCE IN LIGHT OF SCRIPTURE

The Cultural Understanding of Love and Tolerance

In today's society, the concepts of "love" and "tolerance" are often emphasized in ways that may differ significantly from their biblical meanings. Cultural discussions surrounding love often focus on unconditional acceptance and affirmation, while tolerance is commonly understood as accepting all behaviors, regardless of their morality. However, in light of Scripture, love and tolerance are not merely about acceptance without correction or accountability. True love, according to Jesus, involves both compassion and truth, a love that calls people to repentance and transformation. This chapter seeks to define biblical love as demonstrated by Jesus, exploring how it balances grace and truth, and how it impacts modern society.

1. True Love According to Jesus

Jesus' teachings on love provide a comprehensive understanding of love that goes beyond simple affection or emotional warmth. Biblical love is rooted in truth, justice, and correction, alongside mercy and grace. True love, as defined in Scripture, aims for the well-being of others, which often involves guiding people toward righteousness and urging repentance.

- **John 15:13**: *"Greater love has no one than this: to lay down one's life for one's friends."* Jesus defines the ultimate expression of love as self-sacrifice. His willingness to lay down His life for humanity exemplifies sacrificial love, which seeks the ultimate good of others, even at great personal cost.
- **Matthew 22:37-40**: Jesus teaches that the two greatest commandments are to love God and love others. *"Love the Lord your God with all your heart and with all your soul and with all your mind."* And, *"Love*

your neighbor as yourself." This love is comprehensive—loving God fully and loving others selflessly. True love is not self-centered but seeks the good of both God and fellow human beings.

- **Luke 10:25-37 (The Good Samaritan)**: In the parable of the Good Samaritan, Jesus illustrates love through action. The Samaritan demonstrates compassion and love not by offering mere words of comfort, but by going out of his way to help an injured stranger, regardless of cultural differences. This active love is the kind of love Jesus calls His followers to embody.

- **Revelation 3:19**: Jesus demonstrates a crucial aspect of love when He says, *"Those whom I love I rebuke and discipline. So be earnest and repent."* True love is not blind to sin but addresses it, calling people to repentance. In this verse, Jesus links love with correction, revealing that a loving relationship with Him involves recognizing sin and turning from it. This is not a harsh judgment, but a loving invitation to change.

---

2. Love Involves Correction and Repentance

Biblical love is not passive; it actively engages with the moral realities of human life. Jesus demonstrated that love involves not only acceptance but also correction, urging people to repent and live according to God's will. In fact, love without correction is incomplete and lacks the transformative power that God desires for His people.

- **Matthew 18:15-17**: In the context of church discipline, Jesus instructs His followers to approach a fellow believer who has sinned with the goal of reconciliation. *"If your brother or sister sins, go and point out their fault, just between the two of you. If they listen to you, you have won them over."* This process involves a loving confrontation, designed not to condemn, but to restore and heal.

- **2 Timothy 4:2**: Paul, following in Jesus' example, instructs Timothy to *"Preach the word; be prepared in season and out of season; correct, rebuke and encourage—with great patience and careful instruction."* Love requires speaking the truth and addressing sinful behavior, especially within the context of a community of believers. This correction, however, is tempered by patience and care, in order to bring about spiritual growth.

- **Ephesians 4:15**: *"Instead, speaking the truth in love, we will grow to become in every respect the mature body of him who is the head, that is, Christ."* Paul stresses the importance of speaking the truth in love. True love does not ignore truth but speaks it in a way that is compassionate and edifying, with the aim of fostering spiritual maturity.

The biblical understanding of love goes beyond superficial tolerance; it is deeply concerned with the holiness and well-being of others. By calling for repentance, biblical love helps others to grow spiritually and become more like Christ.

---

3. Biblical Love and Tolerance

In contemporary culture, tolerance is often seen as the hallmark of love—accepting others as they are, without challenging their beliefs or behaviors. However, biblical love offers a different perspective. True tolerance, in the biblical sense, involves loving people despite their sins, but also encouraging them to embrace the truth and live according to God's standards. Tolerance, divorced from truth, can lead to moral complacency, whereas love in Scripture never compromises on truth.

- **Romans 1:18-32**: In Romans 1, Paul describes the wrath of God against those who suppress the truth in unrighteousness. He writes that God's judgment is revealed against humanity because of their refusal to acknowledge the truth. This passage shows that true love does not tolerate sin but calls people to repentance and a transformed life.
- **Matthew 7:13-14**: Jesus teaches that the way to eternal life is narrow, and few will find it, while the way to destruction is wide, and many will walk on it. *"Enter through the narrow gate. For wide is the gate and broad is the road that leads to destruction, and many enter through it. But small is the gate and narrow the road that leads to life, and only a few find it."* This highlights the tension between love and tolerance. Love calls people to follow the narrow path of truth, even though the broader, more popular path is the one that leads to destruction.
- **Jude 1:22-23**: Jude encourages believers to show mercy to those who doubt and to save others by snatching them from the fire. While showing mercy, Jude also speaks of the necessity of addressing sin in love, pulling people away from their destructive path. *"To others show mercy, mixed with fear—hating even the clothing stained by corrupted flesh."*

True tolerance, from a biblical perspective, is not about passively accepting all behaviors but actively engaging with people to help them see the truth. It's a love that leads others to repentance, and ultimately, to salvation.

---

4. Positive Impact of Biblical Love on Society

The impact of biblical love extends beyond individual salvation; it transforms communities and societies. When biblical love is practiced, it brings about justice, peace, and a strong sense of moral responsibility. It fosters reconciliation, heals broken relationships, and challenges systemic injustices.

- **Matthew 5:44**: Jesus commands His followers to love their enemies and pray for those who persecute them. *"But I tell you, love your enemies and pray for those who persecute you."* This kind of love, which goes beyond mere tolerance, has the power to transform relationships and communities, breaking cycles of hatred and violence.
- **Galatians 5:22-23**: Paul lists the fruit of the Spirit, which includes love, joy, peace, patience, kindness, goodness, faithfulness, gentleness, and self-control. These virtues contribute to the flourishing of individuals and society as a whole, promoting healthy, loving relationships.
- **James 1:27**: *"Religion that God our Father accepts as pure and faultless is this: to look after orphans and widows in their distress and to keep oneself from being polluted by the world."* Biblical love compels believers to care for the vulnerable and marginalized, showing mercy and justice in a way that uplifts society.

Conclusion: Biblical Love as the Foundation for True Tolerance

In conclusion, biblical love challenges the cultural definitions of tolerance by emphasizing both grace and truth. It does not affirm sin but calls for repentance and transformation. True love, as modeled by Jesus, seeks the well-being of others, even if that involves correction. This love is active, sacrificial, and transformative. It is this love that has the power to positively impact our societies, leading to justice, healing, and reconciliation. Christians are called to embody this love, balancing grace with truth, and speaking the truth in love to a world that desperately needs it.

Transformation vs. Conformity

Introduction: The Battle Between Transformation and Conformity

In today's culture, believers face an ongoing challenge: to remain faithful to biblical principles while living in a society that often promotes values in stark contrast to those outlined in Scripture. The tension between transformation and conformity lies at the heart of the Christian journey. Romans 12:1-2 is a powerful call for believers to embrace a life that is radically different from the prevailing cultural norms. This chapter will explore the distinction between transformation—aligning with God's will—and conformity—being shaped by the world—and how these principles apply to the lives of Christians today.

1. Romans 12:1-2: A Call to Transformation

Romans 12:1-2 provides a profound theological foundation for understanding the Christian's response to the world. Paul exhorts believers to live in a way that reflects the radical change brought about by the gospel. These verses encapsulate the contrast between the transformed life of a believer and the untransformed life of one who conforms to the world's values.

Romans 12:1-2 (NIV):

"Therefore, I urge you, brothers and sisters, in view of God's mercy, to offer your bodies as a living sacrifice, holy and pleasing to God—this is your true and proper worship. Do not conform to the pattern of this world, but be transformed by the renewing of your mind. Then you will be able to test and approve what God's will is—his good, pleasing, and perfect will."

- **"Offer your bodies as a living sacrifice"**: This presents the believer's life as an act of worship, a complete surrender of one's life, including physical actions and decisions, to God. This sacrifice is not a one-time event but a continual dedication to God's purposes.
- **"Do not conform to the pattern of this world"**: The call to resist conformity to the world speaks to the pressure to adopt societal norms, values, and behaviors that oppose God's will. The world often encourages believers to prioritize materialism, self-indulgence, and moral relativism, all of which contradict the principles of Scripture.
- **"Be transformed by the renewing of your mind"**: Transformation involves a radical shift in how we think and perceive the world around us. The renewing

of the mind comes through immersion in God's Word, prayer, and the influence of the Holy Spirit, which empowers believers to think differently from the world.

- **"Then you will be able to test and approve what God's will is"**: When a believer is transformed by the renewing of their mind, they gain the ability to discern God's will in their life. The process of transformation leads to a deeper understanding of what is good, pleasing, and perfect according to God's standards.

---

2. Conformity to the World: A Danger for Believers

Conformity to the world is a subtle yet powerful force that seeks to shape the hearts and minds of believers. In the modern world, the pressures to conform come in various forms: media, cultural trends, peer influence, and even secular ideologies that contradict biblical morality. The world often promotes values such as relativism, secularism, and individualism, all of which clash with God's teachings on holiness, love, and selflessness.

Examples of Cultural Conformity in Today's World:

- **Moral Relativism**: One of the most pressing issues in contemporary society is the rise of moral relativism, where truth becomes subjective. People are encouraged to define what is right for themselves, often disregarding the objective moral standards set forth in Scripture. This aligns with the world's tendency to devalue absolute truth in favor of subjective experience.

- **Sexual Revolution**: In many societies today, traditional views on sexuality have been replaced by cultural movements that promote sexual freedom, redefining marriage, and the acceptance of homosexuality, bisexuality, and transgenderism. The biblical teaching on marriage as a covenant between one man and one woman (Matthew 19:4-6) has become increasingly countercultural. Christians are called to resist this form of conformity by adhering to biblical sexual ethics.

- **Materialism and Consumerism**: The world often values material wealth, success, and status above spiritual values. The pursuit of wealth and comfort can become an idol, overshadowing the call to live simply, generously, and with a heart focused on eternal, rather than temporal, treasures (Matthew 6:19-21).

- **Individualism and Self-Centeredness**: In contrast to the selflessness Jesus advocates (Mark 10:44-45), modern culture exalts individualism and personal fulfillment as the highest goals. Many in society prioritize personal success, comfort, and autonomy over communal responsibility, sacrifice, and humility.

---

3. The Role of the Renewed Mind in Transformation

The renewed mind is at the core of Christian transformation. To resist conformity to the world, believers must undergo a daily process of spiritual renewal, which occurs through the influence of the Holy Spirit and the Word of God. The process of renewing the mind involves intentionally aligning one's thoughts and actions with God's truth, rather than the prevailing societal standards.

- **Philippians 4:8**: Paul encourages believers to think about things that are true, noble, right, pure, lovely, and admirable. *"Whatever is true, whatever is noble, whatever is right, whatever is pure, whatever is lovely, whatever is admirable—if anything is excellent or praiseworthy—think about such things."* This reinforces the idea that the mind must be directed toward godly thoughts, rather than being influenced by worldly patterns.
- **Colossians 3:1-2**: *"Since, then, you have been raised with Christ, set your hearts on things above, where Christ is, seated at the right hand of God. Set your minds on things above, not on earthly things."* The believer is called to set their mind on heavenly realities, which directly challenges the earthly priorities that often dominate society.
- **Romans 8:5-6**: *"Those who live according to the flesh have their minds set on what the flesh desires; but those who live in accordance with the Spirit have their minds set on what the Spirit desires. The mind governed by the flesh is death, but the mind governed by the Spirit is life and peace."* This passage emphasizes the transformative power of the Holy Spirit in renewing the mind. Believers who yield to the Spirit's influence are not subject to the desires of the flesh, but instead, they live according to God's will.

4. Believers Today: In Compliance with Romans 12:1-2

The truth of Romans 12:1-2 is just as relevant for believers today as it was for the early church. Christians are continually confronted with cultural pressures to conform to worldly values. Yet, by God's grace, many are responding to the call of transformation through the renewing of their minds.

- **Engagement with the Word of God**: Many believers today are committed to studying Scripture, which provides the foundation for renewing the mind. Regular reading, meditation, and application of God's Word help Christians resist the pull of cultural conformity. Church communities, Bible studies, and personal devotionals are pivotal spaces for believers to transform their minds and live according to God's truth.
- **Living Counterculturally**: Christians today, through their commitment to biblical values, are often seen as countercultural. They refuse to conform to the moral relativism of the world, choosing instead to stand firm on the biblical teachings about sexuality, marriage, justice, and sanctity of life. Movements such as pro-life advocacy, marriage between one man and one woman, and social justice rooted in Christian principles reflect this resistance to conformity.
- **Spiritual Growth and Discipleship**: Churches are increasingly focused on discipleship programs that encourage transformation over conformity. Programs that help believers grow in Christlikeness—through prayer, community, and service—are essential in shaping the renewed mind.
- **Community Involvement**: Many believers actively work to transform society by influencing culture through education, politics, arts, and business. Rather than passively accepting the status quo, Christians are engaging with society in ways that reflect biblical values, advocating for righteousness, and loving others sacrificially.

Conclusion: The Call to Transformation

The call to transformation in Romans 12:1-2 is not merely a call for personal holiness but a call to live as distinct, redeemed people who reflect God's values in a world that is increasingly hostile to biblical truth. Transformation, by the renewing of the mind, is an ongoing process that empowers believers to live counterculturally, resist conformity to the world, and align their lives with God's perfect will. As believers today embrace this call, they serve as witnesses to the power of the gospel to bring about true change—both in individual lives and in society as a whole.

Balancing Compassion with Truth

Introduction: The Dual Nature of Christian Love

In a world that often emphasizes either unconditional acceptance or strict judgment, Jesus provided a perfect model of love that balances both compassion and truth. His ministry was marked by radical compassion for sinners, yet He never compromised on the truth of God's Word. This chapter will explore how Jesus navigated this delicate balance, offering a model for Christians today to follow in their own interactions with others. By examining Jesus' actions and teachings, we can understand how to approach people with love while still upholding the truth of the gospel.

1. Jesus' Compassion for Sinners

Jesus' earthly ministry was characterized by His profound compassion for people, particularly sinners and outcasts. He consistently reached out to those whom society often rejected, offering them grace, healing, and the opportunity for transformation. His love was not contingent on people's moral perfection, but on their need for salvation and restoration.

Examples of Jesus' Compassion for Sinners:

- **The Woman Caught in Adultery (John 8:1-11):** In this well-known story, a woman is caught in adultery and brought before Jesus by the religious leaders, who ask if she should be stoned according to the Law of Moses. Jesus' response is one of both compassion and wisdom. He tells those without sin to cast the first stone. When no one condemns her, He says, "Neither do I condemn you; go now and leave your life of sin" (John 8:11). Jesus shows mercy to the woman, extending grace without endorsing her sin. His compassion offers hope for transformation, but His command to "leave your life of sin" is a call to repentance, which introduces the other side of the balance: truth.

- **The Tax Collector Zacchaeus (Luke 19:1-10):** Zacchaeus, a tax collector notorious for his greed and dishonesty, climbed a tree to see Jesus as He passed by. Jesus stops, calls him down, and invites Himself to Zacchaeus' house. This act of compassion leads to Zacchaeus' repentance, saying, "Look, Lord! Here and now I give half of my possessions to the poor, and if I have cheated anybody out of anything, I will pay back four times the amount" (Luke 19:8). Jesus affirms Zacchaeus' repentance, showing that His compassion leads to transformation.

- **Healing of the Lepers (Luke 17:11-19):** Jesus heals ten lepers who were cast out by society because of their disease. Despite their physical condition and the social stigma, Jesus heals them, showing His compassion for those on the margins of society. However, Jesus also reminds them of the importance of gratitude and faith (Luke 17:19). This example shows that Jesus did not simply meet physical needs but addressed spiritual issues as well.

---

2. Jesus' Upholding of Divine Truth

While Jesus' compassion was unyielding, He also upheld divine truth without compromise. His message was clear: repentance was necessary for salvation, and God's standards of holiness could not be ignored. He did not overlook sin; rather, He provided a way out through repentance and faith in Him.

Examples of Jesus Upholding Divine Truth:

- **The Sermon on the Mount (Matthew 5-7):** In His famous Sermon on the Mount, Jesus outlines the ethical standards of the Kingdom of God, which are often more demanding than the traditional interpretations of the Mosaic Law. He intensifies moral requirements by addressing the heart and not just outward behavior. For instance, He equates anger with murder and lust with adultery, teaching that God's standards are not only external but also internal. This teaching is rooted in truth, calling for a righteousness that surpasses mere rule-following and seeks purity of heart.

- **Jesus' Teaching on Sin (Matthew 5:29-30):** Jesus does not shy away from confronting sin directly. In Matthew 5:29-30, He warns that if one's eye or hand causes them to sin, it is better to remove it than to be cast into hell. This stark teaching underscores the seriousness of sin and the necessity of dealing with it radically. While Jesus shows compassion to sinners, He never minimizes the gravity of sin. His words are a call to repentance and transformation, highlighting that sin has real consequences.

- **The Rich Young Ruler (Mark 10:17-22):** In the encounter with the rich young ruler, Jesus addresses the man's attachment to wealth, telling him to sell all his possessions and give to the poor in order to follow Him. Jesus' response is a reminder that following Him requires complete surrender. While the man goes away sorrowful, Jesus does not soften the demand for wholehearted devotion. His love for the man is clear, but so is the uncompromising truth that earthly treasures can become idols, hindering one's relationship with God.

---

3. Balancing Compassion and Truth: A Model for Christians Today

Jesus demonstrated that love and truth are not mutually exclusive. Rather, true love always includes the element of truth. In today's world, Christians are called to follow this same pattern: to show compassion without compromising biblical truth. This balance can be difficult, especially in a culture that often prioritizes acceptance over moral standards. However, Christians are not called to simply accept everything or everyone as they are; rather, they are called to love people in a way that invites them to transformation through repentance and faith in Christ.

A. Compassion: Embracing the Broken

Christians must be willing to embrace people where they are—regardless of their sin or brokenness. Whether it's through personal relationships, ministry, or outreach, believers are called to show kindness, empathy, and a willingness to engage with people in their struggles. Compassion involves coming alongside people, offering support, and showing the love of Christ. It is essential for Christians to meet people with open arms, understanding that everyone is in need of grace and redemption.

B. Truth: Calling to Repentance

While compassion is crucial, it must always be accompanied by truth. Jesus never condoned sin, but He called people to repentance, knowing that transformation could only happen when individuals recognized their need for God's grace. In the same way, Christians must not shy away from speaking the truth in love, addressing sin while offering hope for change. The message of the gospel is clear: all have sinned and fall short of the glory of God (Romans 3:23), but through Jesus Christ, forgiveness and new life are possible (John 3:16).

C. The Church's Role in Balancing Compassion and Truth

The church is the community where both compassion and truth should be modeled. Christians are called to be a light to the world, showing the love of Christ through their actions, speech, and attitudes. In church life, this means providing spaces where people can confess their sins, receive counsel, and experience healing and transformation. It also means upholding biblical truth in love, teaching the whole counsel of God's Word without fear of the world's disapproval.

4. Biblical Evidence of Balancing Compassion and Truth

Several passages from Scripture provide guidance on how Christians should balance compassion and truth in their relationships with others:

- **Ephesians 4:15**: *"Instead, speaking the truth in love, we will grow to become in every respect the mature body of him who is the head, that is, Christ."* This passage highlights the need to speak the truth in love, a principle that encompasses both compassion and truth.
- **John 1:14**: *"The Word became flesh and made his dwelling among us. We have seen his glory, the glory of the one and only Son, who came from the Father, full of grace and truth."* Jesus Himself embodies both grace (compassion) and truth, and believers are called to follow His example.
- **1 John 1:9**: *"If we confess our sins, he is faithful and just and will forgive us our sins and purify us from all unrighteousness."* This verse shows that while God is compassionate and willing to forgive, He also requires repentance as part of the process of restoration.

Conclusion: A Call to Christlike Love

Jesus' model of love is a perfect balance of compassion and truth. As His followers, we are called to embrace the broken, extend grace to sinners, and call them to repentance with the same love that Jesus showed. This balanced approach not only leads to genuine transformation but also reflects the heart of God's redemptive plan for humanity. By holding firm to both compassion and truth, Christians can become agents of change in a world desperately in need of both mercy and righteousness.

CHAPTER 07

DOES THE ABASENCE OF EXPLICIT CONDEMNATION IMPLY APPROVAL?

The Challenge of Absence in Scripture

A common argument used to defend certain behaviors, particularly regarding homosexuality, is the claim that the Bible does not explicitly condemn them. This argument suggests that the absence of direct statements condemning homosexuality, for example, implies divine approval or neutrality. However, the interpretation of Scripture involves not only looking at what is explicitly stated, but also understanding the broader principles of biblical morality, the context in which the text was written, and the theological implications of both omission and commission in God's Word.

This chapter seeks to explore whether the absence of an explicit condemnation of a behavior, such as homosexuality, necessarily implies divine approval. Through a careful exegesis of Scripture and an examination of biblical principles, we will explore why silence on specific issues does not automatically translate to approval.

---

1. The Bible's Silence on Certain Issues: Understanding the Context

It is important to recognize that the Bible, while not addressing every conceivable scenario or cultural situation directly, still provides principles for living that can be applied universally. The Bible is a divinely inspired document, and even in areas where direct condemnation or approval is not explicitly mentioned, the underlying moral principles remain clear.

A. The Principle of Moral Continuity:

One of the guiding principles in understanding biblical morality is the continuity of moral law across both the Old and New Testaments. While certain cultural practices and social norms change over time, the moral standards set by God, especially those concerning human nature, creation, and relationships, are enduring.

For example, in the case of marriage, the absence of direct mention of every conceivable marital situation does not mean that any arrangement is acceptable. Jesus, when asked about marriage, pointed to the creation narrative (Matthew 19:4-6), which defined marriage as between one man and one woman. The silence on many variations of marriage throughout the Bible does not mean that all variations are approved, but rather that the foundational principle of marriage as designed by God remains unchanged.

B. Implied Morality in Biblical Principles:

While the Bible may not address every specific behavior directly, its broader teachings set a framework for moral judgment. In Romans 1:18-32, Paul addresses a variety of sinful behaviors and connects them to the rebellion of humanity against God. Even though the letter does not exhaustively list all possible sins, the principles of moral living are established.

The Bible emphasizes the importance of holiness, sexual purity, and obedience to God's laws. In areas where the text is silent, the broader biblical ethical teachings offer guidance. This implies that behaviors which contradict the moral order established by God (e.g., the creation of man and woman in Genesis 1:27 and the law of marriage in Genesis 2:24) cannot be viewed as morally acceptable merely because they are not explicitly condemned.

2. The Absence of Explicit Condemnation: What It Does Not Mean

The absence of explicit condemnation of homosexuality or other behaviors in some parts of the Bible does not automatically translate into divine approval. This silence may be understood in several ways:

A. The Unspoken Assumption of Ethical Standards:

Many biblical authors, especially in the New Testament, operated under the assumption that their audiences understood the moral and ethical standards already established by God in the Old Testament. For instance, in the teachings of Jesus, Paul, and the apostles, certain behaviors were universally recognized as sinful because of the foundational teachings of the Hebrew Scriptures. There was no need to explicitly list every specific sin; the moral code of the Old Testament, including prohibitions against sexual immorality (e.g., Leviticus 18:22), was assumed to be known and understood by the original audience.

In this context, the absence of a specific mention of homosexuality does not imply that the practice was acceptable; rather, it reflects the cultural and theological assumptions shared between the New Testament writers and their audience, which held to the moral law outlined in the Old Testament.

B. The Nature of Biblical Teaching: Indirect Prohibitions and General Principles

In many instances, Scripture provides moral teachings through indirect prohibitions or general principles. For example, while the Bible does not always explicitly mention each sin, it addresses the broader concepts of righteousness, holiness, and God's design for human relationships, thereby implying moral boundaries.

- **Sexual Purity and Holiness**: The Bible emphasizes sexual purity and the importance of adhering to God's design for relationships. Passages such as 1 Thessalonians 4:3-7, where Paul instructs believers to avoid sexual immorality and to honor their bodies as temples of the Holy Spirit, lay down a moral framework that includes both direct and indirect prohibitions. The New Testament does not always specify every kind of sexual immorality, but the principle of sexual purity still applies broadly.
- **Marriage as Between One Man and One Woman**: As previously discussed, the absence of an explicit prohibition against same-sex marriage does not negate the fact that Scripture consistently defines marriage as the union between one man and one woman. Jesus reaffirms this teaching (Matthew 19:4-6), and Paul echoes it in his writings (Ephesians 5:31). Therefore, even without an explicit condemnation of same-sex unions, the definition of marriage according to Scripture provides a boundary that excludes such relationships.

3. The Silence of Scripture as a Call to Be Faithful to God's Design

The Bible's relative silence on some issues, including homosexuality, can be interpreted as a call for believers to remain faithful to the moral and theological principles God has already established. While modern culture may challenge these principles, Christians are called to uphold the standards of Scripture as the foundation for all morality.

A. The Call to Obey God's Original Design:

Jesus frequently pointed His followers back to the original design of creation when discussing moral issues (Matthew 19:4-6, Mark 10:6-9). For example, in Genesis 1:27, God's creation of man and woman in His image establishes the basis for human relationships, including marriage. This foundational principle is echoed throughout the Scriptures and serves as a guiding force for Christian ethics.

Therefore, even in the absence of specific condemnation of certain behaviors, God's original design remains an authoritative source for understanding human sexuality. To reject that design would be to disregard God's intention for human flourishing, as reflected in His creation of male and female and His command for them to be united in marriage.

B. The New Covenant and Its Ethical Demands:

In the New Testament, Jesus and the apostles call believers to live according to the ethical standards of the Kingdom of God, which transcend cultural norms and individual desires. As Christians, we are not to conform to the world's ways but to transform our minds through the renewing power of the Holy Spirit (Romans 12:1-2). This transformation involves living in obedience to God's will, which is revealed through both the specific commands of Scripture and the broader moral principles it presents.

4. Conclusion: Absence Does Not Equal Approval

The absence of explicit condemnation in Scripture should never be interpreted as divine approval. Rather, it often reflects the assumption that God's moral standards, already established in the Old Testament, are well understood and universally applicable. The Bible teaches moral principles that transcend time and culture, and it calls Christians to live according to these principles, whether they are directly stated or implied. Silence on a particular issue, such as homosexuality, does not invalidate God's original design for human relationships or the ethical standards laid out in Scripture. Instead, it is a call to uphold and remain faithful to the clear moral teachings of the Bible, grounded in the Creator's design for human flourishing.

Biblical Authority for Actions (Colossians 3:17)

Introduction: The Importance of Biblical Authority in Christian Living

The question of whether the absence of a direct condemnation by Jesus implies divine approval is often raised in contemporary discussions of morality, especially regarding issues like homosexuality. This chapter will explore this question by examining the authority of Scripture in light of

Colossians 3:17, which instructs believers, "And whatever you do, whether in word or deed, do it all in the name of the Lord Jesus, giving thanks to God the Father through him." This verse establishes the overarching authority of Christ in every area of life, highlighting that all actions—whether explicitly addressed in Scripture or not—must align with the will of God as revealed in His Word.

We will approach this issue through theological, psychological, and philosophical lenses to provide a well-rounded understanding of why the absence of direct condemnation does not necessarily imply divine approval.

---

1. Theological Perspective: Christ as the Ultimate Authority

In Christian theology, the authority of Jesus Christ is central. He is not only the Savior but also the ultimate revelation of God's will (John 1:1, Hebrews 1:2). As the Creator and the one through whom all things were made (John 1:3), Jesus' life, teachings, and actions provide the lens through which all ethical behavior is to be understood. Colossians 3:17 underscores this by placing all human actions under the authority of Christ.

A. Christ's Authority Over Scripture:

While the Gospels do not record every possible sin or action that Christians may face, the authority of Scripture, as inspired by the Holy Spirit, encompasses all aspects of human life. The absence of an explicit condemnation of a particular action does not mean it is permissible. Instead, the broader biblical principles on love, holiness, and righteousness provide clear boundaries. Christ's teachings, such as those in Matthew 5:17-19, where He declares that He did not come to abolish the Law but to fulfill it, show that He did not diminish the moral commands of the Old Testament but affirmed their eternal validity.

In the New Testament, Jesus frequently emphasized the internal motives behind actions, such as the importance of the heart in moral conduct (Matthew 5:21-30). The lack of specific references to every possible sin does not imply approval of every behavior; instead, Jesus' moral teachings provide a foundation on which all behavior must be assessed.

B. The Role of the Apostolic Witness:

After Jesus' ascension, the apostles were entrusted with continuing His mission and teachings. In Colossians 3:17, Paul's call to live in accordance with the authority of Christ reflects the broader apostolic teaching that the Church should submit to the authority of Scripture (2 Timothy 3:16-17). Even where there is no direct statement from Jesus, the apostolic writings, inspired by the Holy Spirit, provide clear guidance on how Christians should live, reinforcing the authority of Christ.

For example, Paul addresses issues like sexual immorality, including homosexual acts, directly (Romans 1:24-27, 1 Corinthians 6:9-11, 1 Timothy 1:10), establishing that they fall outside of God's design for human sexuality. Therefore, the absence of a direct condemnation from Jesus does not indicate approval; it is consistent with the principle that Christ's authority, as mediated through Scripture, governs Christian ethics.

2. Psychological Perspective: Moral Conscience and the Role of Scripture

From a psychological perspective, human beings possess an inherent moral conscience—an understanding of right and wrong, often influenced by culture, upbringing, and personal experiences. While the human conscience is a powerful tool, it is not infallible and can be shaped by various forces, including societal norms and personal desires.

A. Conscience and Moral Decision-Making:

In Romans 2:14-15, Paul explains that even Gentiles who do not have the Law still have the law written on their hearts, suggesting that God has implanted a basic sense of right and wrong in all people. However, as human beings, our conscience can be skewed or dulled by sin, which is why the Bible serves as an objective standard to correct and refine our moral judgments. Colossians 3:17 emphasizes the need to align all actions with the authority of Christ, suggesting that personal conscience must be governed by the objective moral framework established in Scripture.

B. The Role of Scripture in Shaping the Conscience:

When addressing actions that may not be explicitly condemned, Christians are called to apply biblical principles that have shaped and guided moral decision-making for centuries. In matters where the Bible does not provide a direct command, the overall moral framework provided by Scripture still directs Christians toward righteous behavior. In Romans 12:2, Paul encourages believers to "be transformed by the renewing of your mind," emphasizing the ongoing work of Scripture in shaping not only our actions but also our moral consciences.

Psychologically, this means that Christians must continually align their inner moral compass with the teachings of Scripture, even when specific actions or behaviors are not directly addressed. The absence of condemnation in certain areas does not provide a free pass for indulgence, but instead calls for a deeper reliance on the Spirit's guidance through the Word.

---

3. Philosophical Perspective: Ethics Beyond Explicit Command

Philosophically, the absence of explicit condemnation in Scripture invites a discussion on the nature of ethics and moral law. Philosophers have long debated the foundations of morality—whether they are based on divine command, natural law, or human reason. For Christians, the foundation of morality is rooted in the character and will of God, as revealed through Scripture.

A. Natural Law and Moral Order:

From a natural law perspective, which has its roots in the philosophy of Aristotle and has been integrated into Christian thought by figures like Thomas Aquinas, the natural order is seen as a reflection of divine will. The natural law provides a universal standard for right and wrong, which can be discerned through reason and observation of the world. Even in cases where specific behaviors are not addressed in Scripture, the natural law can inform Christian ethics. For example, the design of the human body and the natural function of male and female relationships suggest a teleological (purpose-driven) view of human sexuality that aligns with Scripture's teachings on marriage.

B. Virtue Ethics and the Pursuit of Holiness:

Virtue ethics, another philosophical approach to morality, emphasizes the cultivation of virtues such as love, kindness, patience, and justice. For Christians, these virtues are ultimately rooted in the character of Christ and are essential for living a life that reflects God's holiness (1 Peter 1:16). Even when a specific action is not directly condemned or approved in Scripture, Christians are called to assess their behavior through the lens of virtue—striving to live in accordance with the nature of Christ. This philosophical framework calls believers to continually pursue holiness and righteousness, recognizing that even the absence of direct condemnation requires an adherence to the broader moral framework of God's character.

4. *Conclusion: Biblical Authority and Christian Living*

In conclusion, the absence of direct condemnation by Jesus does not imply divine approval of a behavior. Colossians 3:17 calls all believers to live under the authority of Christ in all things, including areas where Scripture is silent on specifics. Theologically, this means that all actions must be in alignment with God's revealed will, as found in Scripture. Psychologically, Christians are called to align their consciences with the moral principles established in God's Word. Philosophically, the absence of explicit condemnation calls for a deeper understanding of ethics based on natural law and virtue, which guide believers toward holiness.

Ultimately, Scripture provides a sufficient moral framework for believers, and in cases where specific behaviors are not addressed directly, Christians must remain faithful to the principles of righteousness, holiness, and obedience to God's design as revealed in the Bible. The absence of explicit condemnation does not mean approval, but rather, a call to live according to God's moral will, which is perfectly revealed in Jesus Christ.

Silence in Scripture: Clarifying the Importance of Reading Scripture as a Whole

Introduction: Understanding Silence in Scripture

In our study of Scripture, there are instances where God's Word does not explicitly address every issue or moral question we may face in life. Some might interpret this silence as an indication of consent or approval, but a proper understanding of Scripture reveals that silence does not equate to divine approval. The Bible must be interpreted as a whole, and its messages should be understood in light of God's character, revealed will, and moral order.

This chapter explores the theological, biblical, and interpretive importance of reading Scripture holistically, emphasizing that silence in Scripture should not be equated with divine consent. Rather, God's silence must be understood in the context of His overall revelation and moral framework, which speaks to His character, will, and divine justice.

---

1. Theological Foundation: God's Revealed Will and Character

The absence of explicit mention of a particular issue in Scripture is not an endorsement of that issue. Instead, God's silence in some areas must be understood in light of His overall will and the principles that are consistently revealed throughout Scripture. The key to understanding God's will lies in reading Scripture in its entirety, rather than focusing on isolated verses or passages.

A. God's Will as Revealed Through Scripture

Throughout Scripture, we are reminded that God's Word is inspired and authoritative. Paul writes in 2 Timothy 3:16-17, *"All Scripture is God-breathed and is useful for teaching, rebuking, correcting and training in righteousness, so that the servant of God may be thoroughly equipped for every good work."* This means that every part of Scripture contributes to a fuller understanding of God's character and moral order. While individual passages may not address every possible situation or action, the cumulative witness of Scripture gives us a clear understanding of God's will.

B. The Holistic Approach to Scripture

Jesus Himself emphasized the importance of reading Scripture in its entirety and understanding it holistically. In Matthew 5:17, He declared, *"Do not think that I have come to abolish the Law or the Prophets; I have not come to abolish them but to fulfill them."* Jesus affirmed that the moral law and the teachings of the Old Testament continue to hold authority, even if He did not directly address every single detail of life. In the same way, Christians must interpret silence or lack of specific command in light of the broader principles revealed throughout the Bible.

God's moral order is consistent throughout Scripture. For instance, from Genesis to Revelation, we see God's emphasis on the sanctity of marriage, the importance of justice, and the call to holiness. These themes are not only found in the Law of Moses but are reinforced by Jesus and the apostles, even when certain specific sins or behaviors are not directly addressed.

2. *The Role of Silence in Scripture: Does Silence Imply Consent?*

A. Silence as a Reflection of God's Sovereignty

There are times in Scripture when God remains silent, especially in moments where His judgment or actions are not immediately clear. God's silence is not a sign of indifference or approval but rather a reflection of His divine sovereignty. Psalm 50:21 states, *"You thought I was altogether like you, but I will rebuke you and accuse you to your face."* In this passage, God's silence is not to be mistaken for consent; instead, He allows human actions to unfold in order to bring about His ultimate judgment and purpose. Silence should be seen as part of God's sovereign will to allow free will and human responsibility to operate.

B. Silence and the Broader Moral Principles

God's silence on specific actions does not mean those actions are approved, as Scripture frequently establishes general principles that should guide behavior. For example, the Bible does not need to explicitly mention every form of sexual immorality to establish a moral framework for relationships. In Romans 1:26-27, Paul condemns homosexual acts, not through specific mentions of every possible sin, but by appealing to natural law and God's design for human relationships. Paul builds his argument from the created order, which is a reflection of God's will (Romans 1:20). Similarly, in 1 Corinthians 6:9-11 and 1 Timothy 1:10, Paul lists sexual immorality as a sin, relying on broader theological principles rather than direct commands from Jesus.

---

3. The Example of Jesus: Silence Does Not Imply Endorsement

A. Jesus and the Adulterous Woman (John 8:1-11)

One of the most cited examples of perceived divine silence is the account of the woman caught in adultery (John 8:1-11). Jesus did not immediately pronounce a judgment or condemn her but instead invited those without sin to cast the first stone. Some may interpret His silence as indicating tolerance or approval of her sin, but a closer look shows that Jesus did not endorse her actions. Instead, He called her to a life of repentance, saying, *"Go now and leave your life of sin"* (John 8:11). Jesus' silence, in this case, serves to reveal the deeper principles of mercy, forgiveness, and the call to repentance, not moral approval.

B. The Silence of Jesus Before His Accusers (Matthew 27:12-14)

When Jesus stood before Pilate, He remained silent in the face of accusations (Matthew 27:12-14). This silence was not an endorsement of the false charges but a fulfillment of prophecy and a demonstration of His willingness to submit to God's plan of salvation. In a similar way, the absence of explicit statements on certain moral issues does not indicate approval but rather aligns with God's broader redemptive plan and His sovereignty.

4. Reading Scripture Holistically: The Key to Proper Interpretation

The true key to understanding the silence in Scripture is recognizing the need to interpret the Bible as a cohesive whole. The Bible is not a collection of isolated moral commands but a unified revelation of God's will for humanity. For example, while the New Testament may not always repeat the moral prohibitions found in the Old Testament, it consistently reinforces the moral order established in creation, as seen in the teachings of Jesus and the apostles.

A. Jesus' Teachings on the Law

Jesus continually referred to the Old Testament and its moral commands, emphasizing their fulfillment in Him. In Matthew 5:17-20, He stated that the Law would not pass away until it was fulfilled, and He further elaborated that true righteousness surpasses the outward observance of the law. In the same way, Christians must see the teachings of the apostles and the broader biblical narrative as a unified message, where the silence on certain issues does not imply acceptance, but rather underscores the need to live according to God's revealed will in all matters of life.

B. The Principle of Righteousness

The apostle Paul continually speaks to the importance of righteousness in Christian living. In Romans 6:19, he writes,

"I put this in human terms because you are weak in your natural selves. Just as you used to offer the parts of your body in slavery to impurity and to ever-increasing wickedness, so now offer them in slavery to righteousness leading to holiness." Paul's argument is that all actions must conform to the righteous standard established by God, and silence in one area does not exempt believers from this overarching moral framework.

---

5. Conclusion: Silence Should Lead to Reflection, Not Presumption

In conclusion, the silence of Scripture on specific moral issues should never be interpreted as divine consent or approval. God's character, revealed through His Word, consistently calls believers to live according to His moral law and righteousness. Silence must be understood in the broader context of God's redemptive plan, His justice, and His call for repentance.

Therefore, believers must read Scripture holistically, ensuring that every action, even those not explicitly addressed, is brought under the authority of Christ. The absence of a direct statement from Jesus or the apostles does not equate to divine approval. Rather, the entirety of Scripture guides Christians in their moral decisions, always pointing back to God's ultimate revelation of His will through Jesus Christ.

In Colossians 3:17, Paul reminds us that all our actions should be done *"in the name of the Lord Jesus."* This is the true measure of Christian living—aligning all behavior with the character and will of God as revealed through His Word. Silence in Scripture, therefore, should not lead to presumption, but to a deeper reflection on the principles that govern godly living.

Principles from Jesus' Teachings: Guiding Us on Issues He May Not Have Explicitly Addressed

Introduction: The Scope of Jesus' Teachings and Their Continuing Relevance

Throughout His ministry, Jesus gave profound teachings on topics such as marriage, morality, and holiness. While He did not address every possible issue explicitly, His teachings laid down principles that provide guidance for modern believers, even on questions and concerns that were not directly mentioned in Scripture. Jesus' moral and ethical framework, founded on love, purity, justice, and faithfulness to God's will, serves as a guide for how believers should live in response to a world that continually introduces new ethical dilemmas.

This chapter explores the principles from Jesus' teachings and how they offer a moral compass for navigating contemporary issues, including those He may not have directly addressed. By examining key teachings on marriage, morality, and holiness, we can better understand how to apply Jesus' broader theological and ethical principles in areas of life where Scripture may not offer a direct command.

---

1. Jesus' Core Teachings on Marriage: Upholding the Sanctity of the Union

A. Marriage According to Jesus: Genesis and the Created Order

In Matthew 19:3-6, Jesus provides His most direct teaching on marriage when He responds to the Pharisees' question about divorce. He appeals to the creation narrative in Genesis 2:24, saying, *"Haven't you read...that at the beginning the Creator 'made them male and female,' and said, 'For this reason a man will leave his father and mother and be united to his wife, and the two will become one flesh'?"* This foundational principle of marriage—that it is a union between one man and one woman—is central to understanding God's design for marriage.

While Jesus did not directly address every variation of marriage or modern-day relationship structures, His reference to the creation ordinance emphasizes the sanctity and permanence of marriage as a union designed by God. The implication for contemporary discussions on marriage is clear: marriage remains a sacred covenant between one man and one woman, grounded in God's original intent.

B. The Principle of Permanence in Marriage

Jesus' teachings on marriage also emphasize the permanence of the union. In Matthew 19:6, He concludes, *"So they are no longer two, but one flesh. Therefore what God has joined together, let no one separate."* Jesus speaks here not only about the physical union of husband and wife but also the spiritual and emotional bond that God has established in marriage. This principle stands in contrast to modern cultural trends that often treat marriage as a temporary arrangement or one that can be easily dissolved. Jesus calls for a commitment to lifelong faithfulness, which serves as a guiding principle in addressing the sanctity and permanence of marriage in today's world.

2. Jesus' Teachings on Holiness: Living According to God's Will

A. The Call to Personal Holiness and Purity

Jesus consistently taught that following Him required a radical transformation in the lives of His followers. In Matthew 5:27-30, He addresses the issue of adultery, extending the moral command beyond physical acts to include thoughts and intentions. Jesus said, *"But I tell you that anyone who looks at a woman lustfully has already committed adultery with her in his heart."* This passage highlights that holiness is not merely an outward observance of the law but involves the transformation of the heart and mind. Jesus calls His followers to live in purity and holiness, guided by the internal change that comes from a genuine relationship with God.

The principle of holiness applies to a wide range of modern ethical issues. While Jesus did not explicitly address every moral dilemma, He calls His followers to live according to a standard of holiness that reflects God's character. This calls believers to reflect on their thoughts, motivations, and behaviors, ensuring that they align with God's righteousness and purity in every aspect of life.

B. Jesus on the Heart: The Source of Sin and Morality

In Matthew 15:18-19, Jesus explains that what defiles a person comes from the heart, rather than external actions or rituals. He says, *"But the things that come out of a person's mouth come from the heart, and these defile them. For out of the heart come evil thoughts—murder, adultery, sexual immorality, theft, false testimony, slander."* The key takeaway here is that sin begins in the heart and mind, not just in outward actions. Jesus calls His followers to a transformation that begins internally, which has implications for how we think about sin, morality, and purity.

The concept that morality stems from the heart is critical in understanding how Jesus' teachings apply to modern issues. For example, while Jesus may not have explicitly addressed every issue of sexual ethics or social morality, His teachings on the heart set a foundational principle that moral behavior is an outgrowth of inner transformation. This principle guides how Christians can approach contemporary questions in a way that reflects the purity and righteousness of Christ.

3. Jesus' Call to Love: The Guiding Principle for Ethical Decisions

A. The Greatest Commandment: Love God and Neighbor

One of Jesus' most significant ethical teachings is the command to love. In Matthew 22:37-39, Jesus summarizes the law and the prophets in two commands: *"Love the Lord your God with all your heart and with all your soul and with all your mind"* and *"Love your neighbor as yourself."* These commandments encapsulate the essence of Christian morality.

The principle of love, as Jesus defines it, involves selflessness, sacrifice, and concern for the well-being of others. In addressing contemporary moral issues, this call to love should guide the believer's response. Loving others does not mean endorsing sinful behavior, but rather seeking their highest good by upholding biblical truth and promoting righteousness. The application of this principle can guide believers in how to approach issues like homosexuality, marriage, and sexual ethics, ensuring that their actions are motivated by love, truth, and a desire for others to experience the transformative power of Christ.

B. Love and Truth: Balancing Compassion and Correctness

In John 1:14, we learn that Jesus came "full of grace and truth." His example teaches us that love is not mere tolerance but involves both compassion and the courage to speak the truth. This dual emphasis on grace and truth is crucial in responding to contemporary moral issues. While Christians are called to love and accept people as they are, they are also called to uphold the truth of Scripture, which may sometimes challenge societal norms or individual behaviors.

For example, while Jesus' love for the sinner was unconditional, He always called for repentance. In John 8:11, after forgiving the woman caught in adultery, He told her, *"Go now and leave your life of sin."* This example illustrates the need for both love and a call to repentance when engaging with others about moral or ethical issues.

---

4. Jesus' Teachings on Judgment: Righteousness vs. Condemnation

A. The Standard of Judgment

In Matthew 7:1-5, Jesus teaches about judgment: *"Do not judge, or you too will be judged. For in the same way you judge others, you will be judged."* This passage highlights the principle of humility when addressing the faults of others. However, the context of this teaching is important. Jesus was not prohibiting all forms of judgment but warning against hypocritical or harsh judgment. Later, in John 7:24, He says, *"Stop judging by mere appearances, but instead judge correctly."*

Jesus calls His followers to make righteous judgments that are based on truth, not on superficial observations or prejudices. In this regard, Christians must use Scripture as the foundation for evaluating moral actions and should avoid judgments that are unjust or unkind. This principle of righteous judgment shapes how Christians should engage with modern ethical issues, ensuring that their decisions are rooted in truth, mercy, and justice.

5. Conclusion: Principles for Today from Jesus' Teachings

While Jesus did not explicitly address every moral issue in our world today, His teachings on marriage, morality, holiness, love, and judgment provide a clear moral framework that guides believers. By understanding and applying these core principles—faithfulness in marriage, holiness of life, love for others, and the call to righteous judgment—Christians are equipped to navigate complex ethical questions in a way that reflects God's will for their lives.

Ultimately, Jesus' teachings provide timeless principles that transcend specific cultural or societal concerns, calling His followers to live out their faith in a way that honors God and reflects His character. These principles offer moral clarity in a world that is often uncertain and morally conflicted, grounding believers in the unchanging truth of God's Word.

CHAPTER 08

HOMOSEXUALITY IN EARLY CHRISTIANITY AND CHURCH HISTORY

Understanding Homosexuality in Early Christianity

The relationship between Christianity and the issue of homosexuality has been shaped by the teachings of Jesus Christ, the writings of the apostles, and the interpretation of Scripture by church fathers over the centuries. While the specific term "homosexuality" did not exist in the ancient world in the way it is understood today, various forms of same-sex relations were present in the Greco-Roman world, and the early church had to navigate how to address these practices in light of Christian doctrine. This chapter explores the early Christian church's stance on homosexuality, drawing from Scripture, early Christian writings, and historical developments in the church.

1. Biblical Foundation and Early Christian Teachings

The New Testament, particularly in the writings of Paul, offers clear condemnations of same-sex relations. In Romans 1:26-27, Paul writes about individuals exchanging "natural relations" for "unnatural ones," which many scholars understand as a reference to homosexual acts. Similarly, 1 Corinthians 6:9-11 and 1 Timothy 1:9-10 list "men who have sex with men" (often translated as "sodomites" or "effeminate") as part of a broader list of sinful behaviors that prevent individuals from inheriting the kingdom of God.

While the early Christian church did not have a concept of sexual orientation as we understand it today, these passages, along with the broader moral teachings of the Bible, shaped Christian views on sexual morality. The early church, adhering to the principles outlined by the apostles, regarded same-sex sexual activity as sinful, in accordance with both Old Testament laws and the new covenant established by Jesus Christ.

2. Early Christian Writings and the Church Fathers

A. The Apostolic Fathers and Early Christian Writings

In the early centuries of the church, the Apostolic Fathers and other early Christian writers continued to uphold the biblical teachings on sexual morality. The *Didache* (also known as "The Teaching of the Twelve Apostles"), which dates back to the first century, offers moral instructions for Christian living. Although it does not explicitly address homosexuality, it provides a moral framework that condemns sexual immorality broadly. The text specifically condemns adultery, fornication, and other sexual sins, which early Christians understood to encompass same-sex relations.

Similarly, the *Epistle of Barnabas* (2nd century) and writings by Clement of Rome and Ignatius of Antioch emphasize moral purity and adherence to God's commandments. These early Christian writings, while not always explicitly discussing homosexuality, reflect a general opposition to same-sex relations as part of their broader ethical teachings.

B. The Writings of the Church Fathers

Church Fathers such as Augustine, Jerome, and John Chrysostom offer more explicit commentary on homosexuality. Augustine, in his *Confessions* (Book 3), speaks about the sin of lust, which, according to his interpretation, includes same-sex relations. He wrote that lustful desires were an expression of humanity's fallen nature and that Christian sexual ethics called for chastity and the sanctification of desires within the context of heterosexual marriage.

John Chrysostom, one of the most prominent early Christian preachers and theologians, preached vehemently against homosexual acts. In his homilies on Romans, he condemned "unnatural" sexual practices and affirmed that marriage between a man and a woman was the biblical ideal. Chrysostom's writings provide a clear stance against homosexuality, aligning with the broader view of the early church.

Similarly, Jerome, the translator of the Bible into Latin (the *Vulgate*), wrote extensively on moral issues, including sexuality. In his commentary on the book of Galatians, Jerome emphasized that sexual purity was an essential aspect of Christian life and that all forms of sexual immorality, including homosexuality, were incompatible with the kingdom of God.

3. *The Development of Church Doctrine on Homosexuality*

A. The Influence of Roman Law and Societal Norms

In the early centuries of Christianity, the church faced pressures to define its moral teachings not only in relation to Jewish law but also in light of the dominant Greco-Roman culture, which had a different attitude toward sexuality. The Roman Empire, for example, had a complex and varied view of same-sex relationships. While there was a certain level of tolerance for male-male sexual relations, especially among the elite, there was also a growing recognition of the moral failings associated with such acts in early Christian thought.

Early Christian leaders, recognizing the dangers of conforming to pagan values, emphasized that the ethical teachings of the Bible should guide Christian behavior, regardless of the surrounding culture. Consequently, the church upheld the moral standards outlined in Scripture, especially in terms of sexual behavior. Christianity presented a radical departure from the norms of the Roman world, demanding sexual purity and calling for the sanctity of marriage between one man and one woman.

B. The Role of the Church Councils

The early ecumenical councils of the church did not specifically address homosexuality in terms of doctrinal development, but their moral teachings reflect the broader Christian stance on sexual immorality. The *Council of Nicaea* (325 AD), for example, primarily focused on the nature of Christ and the relationship between the Father and the Son. However, subsequent councils and church leaders continued to emphasize the need for moral purity within the Christian community, which included condemnation of same-sex relations as sinful.

By the time of the *Council of Chalcedon* (451 AD), the church had established itself as an authority on Christian ethics, and the moral framework laid down by the Apostles and Church Fathers became the foundation for future Christian teachings on sexuality. These teachings maintained that marriage was between one man and one woman and that sexual purity was an essential aspect of Christian sanctification.

4. The Reformation and Modern Church History

During the Reformation in the 16th century, figures such as Martin Luther and John Calvin emphasized the importance of Scripture and Christian tradition in shaping moral beliefs. Both Luther and Calvin reinforced traditional Christian teachings on sexual morality, upholding the sanctity of marriage and opposing sexual immorality, including homosexuality. Luther, in particular, emphasized that Christian life must be guided by the moral commands of God, which included condemning homosexual acts as sinful.

In the modern era, the issue of homosexuality became increasingly contentious within the church, especially with the rise of secularism and changing social attitudes. Despite cultural shifts, the overwhelming consensus in Protestant and Catholic theology has remained largely consistent, affirming that homosexual behavior is incompatible with biblical teachings on marriage and sexuality.

5. The Church's Ongoing Response to Homosexuality

The response to homosexuality in the modern church has been marked by significant debate. While many mainline Protestant denominations and Catholic institutions have maintained traditional teachings, some liberal factions have begun to advocate for the acceptance of same-sex unions, citing evolving cultural norms and interpretations of Scripture. These views, however, remain contentious and have led to divisions within many denominations.

On the other hand, evangelical and conservative Christian groups continue to uphold the traditional biblical view on marriage, emphasizing that while the church must extend compassion and love to all individuals, it must also call for repentance and sanctification. The Bible's clear teachings on sexual ethics are seen as foundational for the life of the church and the witness of the gospel in the world.

Conclusion: The Legacy of Early Christianity in Shaping the Church's View on Homosexuality

The early Christian church and its leaders laid the foundation for the moral teachings that would shape the church's stance on homosexuality for centuries to come. From the biblical writings of Paul to the theological reflections of the Church Fathers, early Christianity consistently upheld the sanctity of marriage between one man and one woman, rejecting same-sex relations as sinful. While societal attitudes toward sexuality have evolved, the church's historical stance remains rooted in Scripture, offering a moral framework that emphasizes the call to holiness, repentance, and transformation through the power of the gospel.

As contemporary discussions on sexuality continue to unfold, the teachings of early Christianity provide a valuable context for understanding the church's position on homosexuality and its ongoing commitment to upholding biblical moral values.

The Early Church's Stance on Homosexuality

Introduction: The Foundation of Christian Morality

The early Christian church, emerging from the Jewish traditions and teachings of Jesus Christ, was committed to maintaining high standards of moral purity and righteousness. In contrast to the Greco-Roman world, which was known for its sexual freedoms and various expressions of same-sex relations, early Christianity sought to establish a radical ethical framework based on the teachings of Scripture. As a result, the question of homosexuality and its place within Christian morality became a significant issue for the early church.

This chapter explores the early church's stance on homosexuality by examining the views of early Christian leaders, the writings of the church fathers, and the theological foundations of Christian sexual ethics. We will consider the scriptural teachings that shaped these views and explore how the early church confronted the moral issues of their time, including same-sex relationships.

1. The Biblical Foundations of Early Christian Sexual Ethics

The teachings of the early church on homosexuality were rooted in the Scriptures, both Old and New Testament, which provided clear moral directives on sexuality. In the Old Testament, the Mosaic Law explicitly condemns same-sex relations, particularly in Leviticus 18:22 and 20:13. These verses designate male same-sex intercourse as an "abomination" and are understood as clear prohibitions against such acts.

In the New Testament, the Apostle Paul reinforced these Old Testament teachings. In passages such as Romans 1:26-27, 1 Corinthians 6:9-11, and 1 Timothy 1:9-10, Paul described same-sex relationships as unnatural and sinful. Romans 1, in particular, portrays homosexuality as a consequence of humanity's rebellion against God, where individuals "exchanged natural relations for unnatural ones." These passages provided the theological foundation for early Christian teachings on the immorality of homosexual acts.

While the early church was shaped by Jewish moral teachings, it was also deeply influenced by the life and teachings of Jesus Christ. Though Jesus did not directly address homosexuality in the Gospels, His teachings on marriage, purity, and holiness helped to form the basis for Christian moral standards. Jesus affirmed the creation order of marriage between one man and one woman (Matthew 19:4-6), emphasizing the sanctity and permanence of marriage as a divine institution.

2. The Writings of Early Christian Leaders

A. The Apostolic Fathers and Early Christian Writings

The Apostolic Fathers, who wrote during the first and second centuries, did not often address the issue of homosexuality directly. However, their moral instructions reflect the broader sexual ethics of early Christianity, which aligned with the biblical prohibitions against same-sex relations. The *Didache*, an early Christian text dating from the first century, provides moral teachings for the Christian community, condemning fornication and adultery but not explicitly mentioning homosexuality. The absence of direct references to same-sex relations does not indicate approval; rather, it reflects the general stance that sexual immorality was to be avoided.

In *The Epistle of Barnabas*, written around 130 AD, the author exhorts Christians to live lives of holiness and purity. Though there is no explicit reference to homosexuality, the letter condemns idolatry and fornication, both of which were associated with sexual immorality in the broader Roman world. The early Christian texts often addressed sexual ethics broadly, rejecting any form of sexual activity outside the bounds of heterosexual marriage.

B. The Church Fathers and the Theological Interpretation of Scripture

As Christian theology developed in the second and third centuries, church fathers began to offer more explicit condemnations of homosexuality. These early theologians, such as Ignatius of Antioch, Clement of Rome, and Polycarp, upheld the teachings of the apostles regarding marriage and sexual morality, which included the rejection of homosexual practices.

1. John Chrysostom John Chrysostom, one of the most prominent early Christian preachers and theologians, was particularly outspoken on the topic of homosexuality. In his homilies on the Epistle to the Romans, Chrysostom condemned same-sex relations as unnatural and sinful. He argued that such behavior was contrary to God's created order and that Christians must uphold the moral teachings of Scripture. Chrysostom believed that sexual immorality, including homosexuality, was a sign of humanity's fallen nature and that Christians were called to live holy lives in line with God's commands.

2. Augustine of Hippo Augustine, in his work *The City of God* and his *Confessions*, also addressed issues of sexual morality. While Augustine did not specifically focus on homosexuality in his writings, he clearly affirmed that all forms of sexual activity outside of heterosexual marriage were sinful. Augustine's theology of original sin and human sexuality emphasized that human desires were disordered after the Fall, and that chastity and purity were essential for Christians to live out their faith. In his writings, he held to the traditional biblical view that homosexual acts were morally wrong and incompatible with Christian holiness.

3. Jerome Jerome, the translator of the Bible into Latin (the *Vulgate*), also addressed issues of sexual immorality in his writings. In his letters and commentaries, Jerome reiterated the biblical prohibition against homosexual acts and affirmed the sanctity of marriage. His writings reflect the church's consistent stance on sexual ethics, which was based on both the teachings of Jesus and the apostles.

3. The Role of Roman Society in Shaping Early Christian Views on Homosexuality

In the Roman world, same-sex relationships were relatively common, especially among the elite and among soldiers. The practice of pederasty, where older men engaged in sexual relationships with younger boys, was widespread, and the Romans did not have the same moral prohibitions against homosexual acts that early Christians held. The early church, however, viewed such practices as incompatible with the moral order established by God in creation.

As Christianity spread throughout the Roman Empire, the church's teachings on sexual morality came into conflict with the permissive attitudes of the surrounding culture. The church's rejection of same-sex relations, along with its emphasis on monogamous heterosexual marriage, marked a radical departure from the norms of Roman society. The early church saw the sexual ethics of the surrounding culture as a form of idolatry, which led to immorality and spiritual death.

In contrast, Christian ethics emphasized sexual purity as a way to honor God and live according to His will.

4. *The Development of Church Doctrine on Homosexuality*

In the early centuries of Christianity, there was no official church council that specifically addressed homosexuality as a doctrinal issue. However, as Christianity became more institutionalized, the church's moral teachings were formalized through synods, creeds, and the writings of church councils. By the time of the *Council of Nicaea* (325 AD), the church had developed a clear stance on sexual morality, which rejected homosexual acts as sinful.

As Christian teachings spread throughout Europe and into other parts of the world, the early church's teachings on homosexuality were further reinforced by the writings of theologians such as Thomas Aquinas and Martin Luther. These theologians adhered to the traditional biblical understanding of sexuality and continued to uphold marriage between one man and one woman as the only acceptable context for sexual relations.

5. *The Legacy of Early Christian Views on Homosexuality*

The views of the early church on homosexuality have remained influential throughout Christian history, despite shifts in cultural attitudes toward same-sex relationships in modern times. While many modern denominations and Christian groups have begun to debate the issue of homosexuality, the early church's teachings continue to shape the orthodox position of most evangelical, Catholic, and

Orthodox traditions, which continue to hold that homosexual behavior is sinful.

In the face of contemporary debates, the early church's stance on homosexuality serves as a reminder that Christian ethics are rooted in the authority of Scripture, the teachings of Jesus, and the consistent witness of the church throughout history. As such, these teachings continue to provide a framework for understanding Christian sexuality and morality, calling Christians to uphold the biblical vision of marriage and sexual purity.

Conclusion: Upholding Scriptural Truth in the Modern Church

The early Christian church's stance on homosexuality was shaped by Scripture, the teachings of the apostles, and the moral principles established by Jesus Christ. While the specific cultural context of the early church was different from today, the underlying moral principles have remained consistent throughout Christian history. As contemporary debates continue within the church, it is essential to ground our understanding of sexuality in the timeless truth of Scripture, following the example of the early church in upholding the sanctity of marriage between one man and one woman.

Fathers of the Church: Upholding Traditional Sexual Ethics

Introduction: Early Church Fathers and Sexual Ethics

The teachings of the early Church Fathers played a foundational role in shaping Christian theology and ethics, particularly regarding matters of sexuality. As Christianity spread in the Roman Empire, church leaders and theologians were faced with the challenge of defining Christian sexual morality in a culture marked by sexual permissiveness and pagan practices. Among the most prominent of these church figures were **Augustine of Hippo** and **John Chrysostom**, whose writings and sermons continue to influence Christian doctrine today. This chapter will explore how these influential figures upheld traditional sexual ethics, including their teachings on homosexuality, marriage, and chastity, and how their views were shaped by the Bible and the teachings of the apostles.

1. Augustine of Hippo: Defining Christian Sexual Morality

A. Augustine's Theological Context

Augustine, one of the most influential theologians in Western Christianity, provided profound insights into Christian sexual ethics. His writings were shaped by his own personal experiences, his conversion to Christianity, and his deep theological study. Augustine's views on sexuality were heavily influenced by his understanding of **original sin** and the disordered nature of human desires after the Fall.

In his works, Augustine emphasized the importance of chastity, the sanctity of marriage, and the need for sexual relations within the bounds of a marital relationship. He is often cited for his **doctrine of the two purposes of marriage**—procreation and mutual support—both of which align with traditional Christian sexual ethics.

B. Augustine's Stance on Homosexuality

While Augustine did not focus extensively on homosexuality in his writings, his views on sexual immorality are clear. In his monumental work *The City of God* (Book 14, Chapter 24), Augustine draws a sharp contrast between the sexual ethics of the world and the teachings of Christianity. He condemns all forms of sexual immorality, including **adultery, fornication**, and **same-sex relations**, which he viewed as sinful and contrary to God's natural order. Augustine writes:

"The crime of the flesh is rightly punished by the justice of the Creator... For who can doubt that the sin of unnatural lust is rightly condemned, because it is contrary to the order of nature?" (*The City of God*, 14:24).

In line with **Romans 1:26-27**, where Paul condemns same-sex relations as "unnatural" and a result of humanity's rebellion against God, Augustine argued that homosexual acts were a perversion of the natural created order. He understood **sexual desire** as inherently good but distorted by sin. For Augustine, the goal of Christian sexual ethics was not the suppression of desire but its proper orientation within the context of marriage, the only place where sexual activity was permissible.

C. Marriage and Chastity in Augustine's Writings

Augustine's views on marriage were rooted in the Bible's teachings on the sanctity of marriage. In his *Confessions* (Book 9, Chapter 6), Augustine reflects on his past life of sexual promiscuity and his conversion to celibacy. He writes about the **goodness of marriage** but affirms that celibacy, as a higher calling, was the ideal for Christians who could manage their sexual desires.

In *De bono conjugali* ("On the Good of Marriage"), Augustine teaches that marriage should be centered on the pursuit of virtue, and that sexual relations within marriage must be for the purposes of **procreation** and **mutual support**, not for indulgence or sinful lust. **1 Corinthians 7:2-5** supports this view, with Paul encouraging believers to marry in order to avoid sexual immorality but also emphasizing mutual love and respect within the marriage relationship.

2. John Chrysostom: Homosexuality and the Call to Purity

A. John Chrysostom's Background and Influence

John Chrysostom, one of the most prominent Christian preachers and theologians of the fourth and fifth centuries, is often remembered for his eloquent sermons and strong moral teachings. As the Archbishop of Constantinople, Chrysostom's pastoral work was focused on moral reform, particularly in light of the increasingly decadent culture of the Roman Empire. His sermons and writings provide a vivid picture of the early church's stance on sexuality.

B. Chrysostom's Teachings on Homosexuality

Chrysostom, like Augustine, was a firm opponent of homosexuality. In his **Homilies on Romans**, he condemns same-sex relations as unnatural and immoral. He explicitly writes:

"What do you mean by saying, 'I am not ashamed to sin'? In the first place, it is a sin to act thus. And if you will hear me, I will tell you what sin it is: for it is the sin that does not permit us to marry, but works to spoil the nature of things, to destroy the human race, and to confuse the very fabric of creation." (*Homilies on Romans*, Homily 24)

Chrysostom's condemnation of homosexual acts is consistent with the **biblical testimony** that same-sex relations are unnatural and contrary to God's created order. He views homosexuality as a **sinful deviation** from God's design for human sexuality, where the union between a man and a woman reflects the divine intention of procreation and the sanctity of marriage.

Like Augustine, Chrysostom emphasizes that sexual immorality, including homosexuality, is not simply a matter of behavior but reflects deeper **spiritual disobedience** to God. He draws on **Romans 1:26-27** as one of the foundational texts in condemning homosexual behavior, noting that such actions are a result of humanity's rejection of God's moral order.

C. Marriage and Chastity in Chrysostom's Teachings

Chrysostom's teachings on marriage align closely with those of Augustine. He repeatedly stresses the **spiritual** and **theological significance** of marriage as an institution established by God. In his *Homilies on Ephesians*, Chrysostom writes:

"For marriage is not for pleasure, but for bringing forth children... when one marries for the sake of procreation, and according to God's order, there is no sin. But if marriage is contracted for pleasure, it becomes a sin."

In line with **Genesis 2:24** and **Ephesians 5:31**, Chrysostom affirms that marriage is a sacred covenant between a man and a woman, which is intended not only for mutual support but also for the procreation of children and the continuation of human life. He emphasizes the importance of **sexual purity** within marriage, urging married couples to uphold God's standards and avoid sinful indulgence.

3. Biblical Evidence Supporting Their Teachings

Both Augustine and Chrysostom's views on homosexuality are rooted in the **biblical teachings** that reflect God's design for sexuality. Several key scriptures undergird their theological positions:

- **Romans 1:26-27**: Paul's condemnation of same-sex relations as "unnatural" and "against nature" serves as a cornerstone for both Augustine and Chrysostom's understanding of homosexuality as a sinful act.
- **1 Corinthians 6:9-10**: Paul's list of sins that exclude people from the kingdom of God includes "men who have sex with men" (NIV), reinforcing the early Christian rejection of homosexual behavior.
- **Genesis 2:24**: The establishment of marriage between a man and a woman as a divine institution serves as a basis for the church fathers' teachings on the sanctity of marriage and the natural order of human sexuality.
- **Ephesians 5:31-32**: Paul's affirmation of the union of man and woman in marriage highlights the theological significance of marriage and its role in reflecting the image of Christ and the Church.

4. Conclusion: The Enduring Legacy of Early Christian Teachings

The teachings of **Augustine** and **John Chrysostom** laid a strong theological and moral foundation for Christian sexual ethics. Their emphasis on the biblical understanding of marriage, sexual purity, and the sinfulness of homosexual behavior has had a profound influence on the Christian tradition. While modern debates about sexuality may present challenges to traditional views, the early church's stance on these issues remains an important guide for Christians seeking to understand and live according to God's design for human sexuality.

Consistency Across Christian Doctrine: Sexual Ethics from Jesus to the Apostolic Church and Beyond

Introduction: The Unchanging Teachings on Sexual Morality

Christian sexual ethics have remained remarkably consistent from the teachings of Jesus Christ, through the apostles, and into the history of the Church. The continuity of these teachings on marriage, morality, and sexual ethics has not only shaped Christian communities but has also provided a framework for understanding the sanctity of human sexuality. This chapter will explore how the principles of sexual morality articulated in the New Testament and upheld by early Christian leaders have been passed down throughout Christian history. We will also examine how these teachings continue to influence Christian societies today, and consider whether the modern, secular world can adopt or engage with these biblical principles.

1. Jesus' Teachings on Sexual Morality

Jesus' teachings on sexual morality are often more implicit than explicit but are nevertheless foundational for Christian ethics. Jesus upheld the sanctity of marriage and emphasized purity in thought and action. His teachings, particularly in the Gospels, align with the creation narrative in **Genesis 2:24**, where marriage is defined as a sacred union between a man and a woman. In **Matthew 5:27-28**, Jesus raises the bar of sexual morality beyond outward behavior to include inner thoughts and desires:

"You have heard that it was said, 'You shall not commit adultery.' But I tell you that anyone who looks at a woman lustfully has already committed adultery with her in his heart."

Here, Jesus deepens the ethical standard by calling for purity of heart and mind, showing that sexual sin begins not just with actions but with desires. His stance on marriage, **sexuality**, and **morality** is in direct continuity with the Jewish laws and teachings, reinforcing God's original design for human relationships. While Jesus did not explicitly address homosexuality, His affirmation of traditional marriage (Matthew 19:4-6) sets the stage for the consistent teachings of the apostles and early Church Fathers on sexual ethics.

2. Apostolic Teachings on Sexual Morality

Following Jesus, the apostles of the early Church continued to uphold the teachings on sexual morality with clear instructions to the Christian community. In **1 Corinthians 6:9-11**, Paul writes:

"Or do you not know that wrongdoers will not inherit the kingdom of God? Do not be deceived: neither the sexually immoral nor idolaters nor adulterers nor men who have sex with men... will inherit the kingdom of God."

This passage, along with other letters, reflects the continuity of **biblical sexual ethics**, including the rejection of homosexuality and other forms of sexual immorality. Paul affirms that sexual purity is essential for salvation and that those who persist in such behaviors without repentance are outside the kingdom of God. Similarly, in **Romans 1:24-27**, Paul explicitly condemns homosexual acts as unnatural, a judgment that echoes the Old Testament prohibitions in **Leviticus 18:22** and **20:13**.

Moreover, the apostolic writings emphasize **marriage** as a sacred covenant between one man and one woman, following the example set in **Genesis 2:24**. In **Ephesians 5:31-32**, Paul reiterates this, calling marriage a profound mystery that symbolizes the relationship between Christ and the Church. The apostolic teaching reflects Jesus' own understanding of marriage, ensuring that the church's sexual ethics would remain consistent with its theological foundations.

3. The Early Church Fathers and the Continuity of Sexual Ethics

The early Church Fathers, such as **Augustine of Hippo** and **John Chrysostom**, were deeply committed to upholding biblical sexual morality. They did not deviate from the teachings of Jesus and the apostles but instead expounded on them in response to the challenges posed by the surrounding culture.

- **Augustine of Hippo** wrote extensively on the sanctity of marriage, the dangers of fornication, and the inherent sinfulness of homosexual acts. He upheld the idea that sexual desire, while natural, must be properly ordered within the confines of marriage between a man and a woman, and that any other expression of sexuality outside of marriage was sinful.

- **John Chrysostom** similarly condemned all forms of sexual immorality, including homosexuality, affirming the biblical view that marriage is a sacred institution intended for procreation and mutual support between a man and a woman.

The writings of these early Church Fathers, alongside the New Testament teachings, set a clear and consistent foundation for Christian sexual ethics that extended into the medieval period and beyond. **Theological consistency** across centuries shows that the Church has maintained its stance on issues of sexual morality in alignment with biblical principles.

4. *The Influence of Christian Sexual Ethics in Modern Society*

The continuity of Christian sexual ethics from Jesus to the apostles, and through the Church Fathers, has had a profound influence on Western societies. Throughout history, Christian teachings on marriage, family, and sexuality have shaped cultural norms, legal systems, and social expectations. For instance, the Christian concept of **monogamous marriage** became the standard in Europe, influencing laws around marriage, inheritance, and family life.

In the modern era, however, these teachings have faced significant challenges due to the rise of secularism, postmodernism, and changing social attitudes toward marriage and sexuality. Issues such as divorce, homosexuality, cohabitation, and gender identity have increasingly become subjects of public debate and legal redefinition. While many Christian communities continue to uphold traditional sexual ethics, mainstream culture, particularly in Western nations, has seen a shift towards greater acceptance of diverse sexual expressions and relationships outside of the biblical model.

Despite this shift, **Christian societies** still hold to traditional views on marriage and sexuality, though these views are often marginalized or challenged in secular spaces. Many churches, especially those within conservative denominations, continue to uphold the biblical stance on sexual morality, advocating for **sexual purity**, **marital fidelity**, and the **sanctity of marriage**. These teachings influence the **ethical framework** of Christian communities and shape their responses to social and political issues.

5. Can the Circular World Adopt Biblical Sexual Ethics?

As society continues to move away from biblical norms and embraces a more permissive view of sexuality, the question arises: Can a secular, pluralistic society adopt or even engage with Christian sexual ethics?

From a **theological perspective**, the answer is yes—but with important distinctions. Christianity teaches that God's design for human sexuality is not only for the benefit of individual believers but also for the flourishing of society as a whole. Biblical sexual ethics encourage **healthy relationships**, the **well-being of families**, and the **protection of children**. The biblical view on marriage promotes stability and provides a clear structure for relationships, which can be beneficial for society as a whole.

From a **psychological perspective**, embracing traditional sexual ethics may contribute to **mental health** and **emotional stability**. Studies have shown that children raised in stable, two-parent households tend to thrive emotionally and socially. Traditional Christian views on marriage, based on **commitment**, **self-sacrifice**, and **faithfulness**, contribute to the flourishing of individuals and communities. However, the modern secular worldview, with its emphasis on individual freedom and self-expression, often conflicts with these values.

From a **philosophical perspective**, the question of whether secular society can adopt biblical sexual ethics hinges on the recognition of objective moral values. If one believes in **moral relativism**, the teachings of Christianity on sexual morality may seem out of place. However, if one believes in **objective moral truths**—which many Christians argue are inherent in the created order—then adopting biblical sexual ethics can be seen as beneficial for human flourishing, irrespective of one's religious beliefs.

6. Conclusion: A Consistent Biblical Ethic for Today

The continuity of Christian sexual ethics, from Jesus' teachings to the apostolic Church and through the centuries, provides a stable foundation for believers today. While secular society has increasingly moved away from biblical standards, Christian communities continue to uphold the biblical model of marriage and sexuality, which serves not only to protect individuals but also to nurture the health of society as a whole.

Whether or not the broader secular world can adopt these teachings remains uncertain, but the call for repentance, transformation, and adherence to God's will for human sexuality continues to be a central tenet of the Christian faith. The enduring nature of biblical sexual ethics stands as a testimony to God's design for humanity, and those who choose to embrace this moral framework find not only spiritual growth but societal stability and personal fulfillment.

149

CHAPTER 09

REDEMPTION, REPENTACE, AND TRANSFORMATION

Jesus' Call to Repentance

The ministry of Jesus Christ was not just one of miraculous healings and teachings; it was fundamentally centered on the call to repentance. Repentance, as a key element of the gospel message, reflects the heart of Jesus' mission to restore humanity to a right relationship with God. In this chapter, we will explore the nature of repentance, how Jesus called sinners to turn from their ways, and the transformative power that comes through repentance, particularly in the context of redemption.

1. The Nature of Repentance in Jesus' Ministry

Repentance, in the biblical sense, involves a deep and sincere turning away from sin and a return to God. This is not just a change in outward behavior, but a radical shift in the heart, mind, and soul. The word *repent* comes from the Greek term *metanoia*, meaning "to change one's mind" or "to have a change of heart." Jesus used this concept throughout His ministry, calling people to abandon sinful ways and to live in alignment with God's will.

In **Matthew 9:13**, Jesus makes it clear that His mission is not to call the righteous but the sinners to repentance:

"But go and learn what this means: 'I desire mercy, not sacrifice.' For I have not come to call the righteous, but sinners."

This passage demonstrates that Jesus came to engage with the lost and broken, not with those who were self-righteous. His message was to the people who recognized their need for forgiveness and transformation. Jesus was not simply calling people to a moral reformation but to a radical spiritual change that would lead to salvation.

2. Repentance and Redemption: The Heart of Jesus' Ministry

The call to repentance is closely tied to the message of redemption. Redemption in the New Testament refers to the act of being freed from the bondage of sin and restored to a right relationship with God. Jesus' entire ministry was built on the concept of redemption through repentance. Without repentance, there could be no genuine redemption, as it is the key that opens the door to forgiveness and a new life in Christ.

In **Luke 5:32**, Jesus reiterates this idea:

"I have not come to call the righteous, but sinners to repentance."

Here, Jesus emphasizes that repentance is the first step in receiving His grace and entering into the redemptive work He offers. This is the essence of the gospel message: repentance leads to forgiveness, which in turn leads to salvation. Without this repentance, the redemptive power of Christ's death and resurrection cannot be fully realized in an individual's life.

Acts 3:19 further emphasizes this:

"Repent, then, and turn to God, so that your sins may be wiped out, that times of refreshing may come from the Lord."

This call highlights that repentance is not merely a sorrow for sin, but an active turning to God in faith. Through this turning, sins are forgiven, and the believer experiences spiritual renewal. The act of repentance in the New Testament is often portrayed as part of a process of salvation—a turning from the old self and a movement towards the new life found in Christ.

3. The Transformative Power of Repentance

Repentance is not a one-time event; it is a continual process of transformation. Jesus did not simply call people to repent once and then continue living as they had before. He invited them to live lives marked by ongoing transformation. In **Matthew 4:17**, at the beginning of His ministry, Jesus proclaimed:

"Repent, for the kingdom of heaven has come near."

This call was not only a message about salvation but also a call to live under the reign of God's kingdom, where sin is replaced by holiness and self-centeredness is replaced by a heart for others. Repentance, then, is the pathway through which transformation occurs—both in the heart and in behavior.

Romans 12:1-2 speaks to this transformative power of repentance in the believer's life:

"Therefore, I urge you, brothers and sisters, in view of God's mercy, to offer your bodies as a living sacrifice, holy and pleasing to God—this is your true and proper worship. Do not conform to the pattern of this world, but be transformed by the renewing of your mind. Then you will be able to test and approve what God's will is—his good, pleasing and perfect will."

This passage shows that repentance, which involves the renewal of the mind and the surrender of one's life to God, leads to a transformation that aligns a believer's will with God's. It is a continual process of sanctification, where the believer is changed by the power of God to reflect His holiness more each day.

4. Jesus' Call to Repentance and the Power of Grace

It is important to note that Jesus' call to repentance is not a harsh demand but an invitation to experience God's grace. **Repentance is never meant to be a burden** but a doorway to a life of forgiveness and peace. Jesus' compassion and love for sinners were evident in how He approached them. For example, when Jesus encountered the woman caught in adultery, He did not condemn her but called her to repentance:

"Go now and leave your life of sin." (John 8:11)

This statement exemplifies the balance of grace and truth that Jesus brought—He did not condone sin, but He offered forgiveness and the opportunity for transformation. Jesus' call to repentance was not about condemning sinners but about offering them a path to healing and restoration.

The invitation to repentance is also extended in **Revelation 3:19**, where Jesus, speaking to the Church of Laodicea, says:

"Those whom I love I rebuke and discipline. So be earnest and repent."

This verse shows that Jesus' discipline and call to repentance are acts of love. He desires transformation, not judgment, and invites His followers into a life that reflects His love, holiness, and righteousness.

5. *Repentance in the Christian Life: Ongoing and Transformative*

Repentance is not something that is only needed at the point of salvation; it is an ongoing process throughout the Christian life. Christians are called to continually turn from sin and seek God's forgiveness and cleansing. This ongoing repentance is rooted in the reality of the believer's relationship with Christ.

The apostle **John** writes in **1 John 1:9**:

"If we confess our sins, he is faithful and just and will forgive us our sins and purify us from all unrighteousness."

This ongoing process of repentance is part of the believer's sanctification. It is a daily turning to God, confessing sins, and receiving His grace and forgiveness. The more the believer grows in their relationship with Christ, the more they become aware of areas of their life that need transformation, leading them to repentance.

6. *Repentance and the Hope of Redemption*

Jesus' call to repentance is filled with hope. The central message of His life and ministry was that repentance leads to redemption—a complete reversal of the consequences of sin and a restoration of the individual to a right relationship with God. The hope of redemption is not just a future promise but a present reality that begins in the here and now.

Romans 8:1 gives assurance to those who repent and turn to Christ:

"Therefore, there is now no condemnation for those who are in Christ Jesus."

Repentance does not only remove the penalty of sin but brings about a restored relationship with God, peace, and the indwelling presence of the Holy Spirit. Through Christ, the power of sin is broken, and the redeemed believer can live a life marked by holiness, purpose, and transformation.

7. Conclusion: The Ongoing Call to Repentance and Redemption

The call to repentance is not merely a call to abandon sin but an invitation to a life of transformation, redemption, and restoration through Jesus Christ. Repentance is the pathway to forgiveness and renewal, and through it, the believer experiences the full scope of God's grace. Jesus' ministry was centered on this call to repentance, and it remains central to the message of the gospel today. It is not merely about feeling sorry for one's sin, but about turning to God in faith, allowing His grace to transform and redeem. Through repentance, believers can experience the fullness of God's love, power, and forgiveness, living lives that reflect the holiness and righteousness of God.

Salvation for All: Christ's Offer of Redemption

Introduction

Salvation through Jesus Christ is a universal invitation, available to all who are willing to repent and embrace the transformative power of the gospel. This includes individuals who have engaged in lifestyles or behaviors that the Bible condemns, including homosexuality. The message of salvation is not exclusive or limited by past actions or sins, but is an invitation to every person, regardless of their past, to experience forgiveness, healing, and new life in Christ. This chapter will explore the profound truth that salvation is for all, including those who have practiced homosexuality, and emphasize the critical role of repentance and obedience in accessing this grace.

1. Christ's Salvation: A Universal Invitation

The central message of the gospel is that Christ's salvation is available to all humanity, regardless of sin or past behavior. Jesus came to seek and save the lost (Luke 19:10), and His sacrifice on the cross provides redemption for every person. This includes those who have engaged in sexual sin, including homosexuality, and all other sins.

In **Matthew 11:28-30**, Jesus extends an open invitation to all who are weary and burdened:

"Come to me, all you who are weary and burdened, and I will give you rest. Take my yoke upon you and learn from me, for I am gentle and humble in heart, and you will find rest for your souls."

This passage reflects the heart of Jesus' ministry—an offer of rest, peace, and healing for all people, regardless of the sins they have committed. The salvation offered by Christ is not for a select few, but for all who are willing to repent and trust in Him.

The apostle **Paul** reaffirms this message in **1 Timothy 2:3-4**:

"This is good, and pleases God our Savior, who wants all people to be saved and to come to a knowledge of the truth."

God desires that all people come to repentance and be saved. This is the inclusive nature of Christ's salvation—He does not wish for any person to perish, regardless of their background, struggles, or sins.

2. Repentance as the Pathway to Salvation

While salvation is available to all, it is only accessible through repentance. **Repentance** is a turning away from sin and a turning toward God. It is not a superficial apology but a deep, heart-felt transformation that affects one's mind, will, and actions. In **Acts 3:19**, the apostle **Peter** urges those who hear the gospel to:

"Repent, then, and turn to God, so that your sins may be wiped out, that times of refreshing may come from the Lord."

Repentance is the first step in receiving the forgiveness and grace of Christ. It involves acknowledging one's sin, turning away from that sin, and choosing to follow Christ in obedience. This is a critical aspect of salvation because without repentance, there can be no forgiveness. Repentance is not just an acknowledgment of wrong, but an active choice to change one's life in obedience to God.

1 John 1:9 offers the hope of forgiveness to all who repent:

"If we confess our sins, he is faithful and just and will forgive us our sins and purify us from all unrighteousness."

This promise is open to everyone, including those who have practiced homosexuality. The key to receiving this forgiveness is repentance and turning to Christ. Jesus' death on the cross made forgiveness available to all, but it is only effective when a person chooses to repent and believe in Him.

3. Homosexuality and the Need for Repentance

The Bible consistently teaches that homosexual behavior is a sin (Romans 1:26-27, 1 Corinthians 6:9-10), but it also teaches that **repentance** is the way out of sin and into freedom. **1 Corinthians 6:9-11** is particularly significant in this context:

"Or do you not know that wrongdoers will not inherit the kingdom of God? Do not be deceived: neither the sexually immoral nor idolaters nor adulterers nor men who have sex with men nor thieves nor the greedy nor drunkards nor slanderers nor swindlers will inherit the kingdom of God. And that is what some of you were. But you were washed, you were sanctified, you were justified in the name of the Lord Jesus Christ and by the Spirit of our God."

This passage clearly affirms that homosexual acts are sinful, but it also provides hope. It reminds the Corinthians (and all readers) that they were once lost in sin, but through repentance, they were washed, sanctified, and justified by Christ. This same hope is available today for those who struggle with any sin, including homosexuality. Through repentance, they can experience the transformation that Christ offers.

4. The Power of Redemption

One of the most beautiful aspects of Christ's offer of salvation is that it is **transformative**. The message of redemption is not that God simply forgives sin but that He **transforms lives**. This is made clear in **2 Corinthians 5:17**, where Paul writes:

"Therefore, if anyone is in Christ, the new creation has come: The old has gone, the new is here!"

This new creation is not merely a change of behavior; it is a complete transformation of the heart and mind. When a person comes to Christ in repentance, they are made a new creation—able to live a life of holiness and obedience to God. For those who have struggled with homosexuality, this transformation is no different. The same power that raised Jesus from the dead is available to those who repent and believe in Him, enabling them to overcome sin and walk in newness of life.

In **Titus 3:5**, Paul reminds believers that salvation is not by our own works but by the mercy of God:

"He saved us, not because of righteous things we had done, but because of his mercy. He saved us through the washing of rebirth and renewal by the Holy Spirit."

The Holy Spirit empowers believers to live according to God's will, and through the Spirit, individuals who have struggled with homosexuality can experience true transformation. This is not a process of behavior modification but a spiritual renewal that brings lasting change.

5. Salvation Is a Call to Holiness

Repentance and salvation are not merely about escaping judgment but about **entering into a life of holiness**. The Bible makes it clear that Christians are called to live according to God's will and to pursue righteousness. In **1 Peter 1:15-16**, Peter writes:

"But just as he who called you is holy, so be holy in all you do; for it is written: 'Be holy, because I am holy.'"

Holiness is the fruit of genuine repentance and salvation. When individuals come to Christ, they are called not only to leave their old lives of sin behind but to live lives that reflect God's holiness. This involves forsaking all sinful behaviors and walking in obedience to God's commands, including those related to sexuality.

For those who have engaged in homosexual behavior, the call is the same. The grace of God extends to all, but this grace is not meant to leave a person in their sin; it is meant to bring about holiness and transformation. **1 Thessalonians 4:3-7** affirms that God's will for His people is sanctification—being set apart from sin and living in holiness.

6. Conclusion: Salvation and Transformation for All

Christ's offer of salvation is truly for all people. Regardless of one's past, including involvement in homosexual behavior, the gospel extends the invitation of forgiveness, redemption, and transformation. Salvation is not simply about escaping the consequences of sin but about embracing a new life in Christ—one that is characterized by repentance, holiness, and the ongoing work of the Holy Spirit.

Through repentance and faith in Jesus Christ, individuals who have practiced homosexuality can be transformed and walk in the newness of life that Christ offers. There is no sin too great for God's grace, and His invitation to salvation is open to all who will come to Him in humility and obedience. This is the hope of the gospel: **"For everyone who calls on the name of the Lord will be saved"** (Romans 10:13).

The Hope of Transformation

Introduction

The gospel message is one of profound hope and transformation. It offers a way out of the bondage of sin, a path to new life, and a promise of complete renewal through the power of the Holy Spirit. In Christ, no one is beyond redemption. The gospel does not just promise forgiveness but also the power to live a transformed life, aligned with God's will. This chapter explores how the gospel offers hope and transformation, emphasizing that through repentance, faith, and obedience to God's Word, believers are enabled to live according to God's standard of holiness.

---

1. The Gospel: A Message of Hope

At the heart of the gospel is the offer of hope—a hope that sinners can be redeemed and transformed by the power of God's love and grace. **Ephesians 2:4-5** encapsulates this message:

"But because of his great love for us, God, who is rich in mercy, made us alive with Christ even when we were dead in transgressions—it is by grace you have been saved."

This passage reveals the transformative power of God's love and mercy. The message of salvation is not just about escape from judgment but about being made spiritually alive in Christ. Apart from Christ, we were dead in sin, but through His grace, we are made alive, offering believers a fresh start, a new identity, and a restored relationship with God.

Romans 5:8 reinforces this truth, declaring:

"But God demonstrates his own love for us in this: While we were still sinners, Christ died for us."

Christ's sacrificial death on the cross represents the ultimate demonstration of God's love for humanity. The hope of the gospel is grounded in this act of grace and is extended to all people, no matter their past. The transformative power of the gospel is rooted in the fact that Christ died for sinners, offering them the opportunity for renewal, healing, and wholeness.

2. Transformation in Christ

The gospel calls for more than just a change of behavior; it invites individuals into a radical transformation of the heart and mind. **2 Corinthians 5:17** captures this truth:

"Therefore, if anyone is in Christ, the new creation has come: The old has gone, the new is here!"

This verse illustrates the nature of transformation that occurs when a person becomes a believer. It is not a mere adjustment of one's actions or habits, but a fundamental change in one's identity. The moment a person accepts Christ, they are made into a new creation—born again and empowered by the Holy Spirit to live in a way that pleases God.

This transformation is the result of the **sanctifying work** of the Holy Spirit. **Titus 3:5** affirms that salvation involves renewal by the Holy Spirit:

"He saved us, not because of righteous things we had done, but because of his mercy. He saved us through the washing of rebirth and renewal by the Holy Spirit."

The Holy Spirit is instrumental in this transformation process. Through His work, believers are gradually conformed to the image of Christ, empowered to overcome sin and live in obedience to God. The transformation is not instantaneous but progressive, as the believer grows in holiness and maturity, living more fully in line with God's Word.

3. The Call to Repentance and Renewal

Transformation begins with repentance. **Repentance** is a turning away from sin and a turning toward God. It is the first step in experiencing the hope of transformation that the gospel offers. **Acts 3:19** calls all people to repentance:

"Repent, then, and turn to God, so that your sins may be wiped out, that times of refreshing may come from the Lord."

Repentance is essential because it opens the door for the work of transformation to begin. When an individual repents, they acknowledge their sin and surrender to God's will, allowing the Holy Spirit to begin His work of renewal.

Romans 12:1-2 emphasizes the ongoing nature of transformation:

"Therefore, I urge you, brothers and sisters, in view of God's mercy, to offer your bodies as a living sacrifice, holy and pleasing to God—this is your true and proper worship. Do not conform to the pattern of this world, but be transformed by the renewing of your mind. Then you will be able to test and approve what God's will is—his good, pleasing, and perfect will."

This passage outlines two important aspects of transformation: presenting our lives as living sacrifices and undergoing the renewal of our minds. Transformation is a continuous process that involves surrendering every area of life to God's control and allowing the Holy Spirit to renew our minds and hearts. As our minds are renewed, we become more aligned with God's will, and our lives begin to reflect His holiness.

4. Living in Obedience to God's Word

Transformation is also characterized by a life of **obedience** to God's Word. The Bible teaches that genuine faith is demonstrated through actions. **James 2:26** makes it clear:

"As the body without the spirit is dead, so faith without deeds is dead."

Obedience is the natural outflow of a transformed life. **1 John 2:3-6** stresses that those who claim to know Christ must walk in obedience to His commands:

"We know that we have come to know him if we keep his commands. Whoever says, 'I know him,' but does not do what he commands is a liar, and the truth is not in that person. But if anyone obeys his word, love for God is truly made complete in them. This is how we know we are in him: Whoever claims to live in him must live as Jesus did."

Living in obedience to God's Word is evidence of genuine transformation. The gospel not only offers forgiveness for past sins but also calls believers to live according to God's standards. As believers allow the Holy Spirit to work in their lives, they are empowered to obey God's Word, even in areas that challenge them.

5. *The Power of Transformation for Overcoming Sin*

The power of the gospel to transform lives is particularly evident in overcoming persistent sins. **Romans 6:6-7** declares:

"For we know that our old self was crucified with him so that the body ruled by sin might be done away with, that we should no longer be slaves to sin—because anyone who has died has been set free from sin."

Christ's death and resurrection set believers free from the power of sin. Through His work, Christians are no longer slaves to sin but are empowered to live in righteousness. This includes victory over all types of sin, including sexual sin. Transformation is not only about changing outward behavior but also about being freed from sin's grip and living in the power of the Holy Spirit.

1 Corinthians 10:13 offers additional encouragement:

"No temptation has overtaken you except what is common to mankind. And God is faithful; he will not let you be tempted beyond what you can bear. But when you are tempted, he will also provide a way out so that you can endure it."

Through the power of the Holy Spirit, believers have the strength to resist temptation and to live in obedience to God's will. The transformation that the gospel brings enables believers to overcome even the most challenging temptations, living victoriously in Christ.

6. Conclusion: The Ongoing Hope of Transformation

The gospel offers both **hope** and **transformation** to all who believe. This is not a hope based on wishful thinking, but a transformative power that changes hearts, minds, and lives. Through repentance, faith, and the ongoing work of the Holy Spirit, believers can experience victory over sin and begin to live according to God's will.

As we surrender to God's Word, live in obedience, and allow the Holy Spirit to renew our minds, we reflect Christ's character in our lives. This transformation is both a present reality and a future hope, as we look forward to the day when we will be fully conformed to the image of Christ. The hope of transformation is not limited by past sin or failures but is available to all who come to Christ, repent, and follow Him.

In conclusion, the gospel is a message of hope and transformation, offering the power to overcome sin, live in holiness, and reflect God's glory in every aspect of life. This message is for all, regardless of their past, and it calls each of us to live in the newness of life that Christ offers. Through the gospel, we can be assured that the hope of transformation is a present reality and a future promise.

CHAPTER 10

PRACTICAL GUIDANCE FOR CHRISTIANS ON RESPONDING TO CULTURAL SHIFTS

In the midst of rapid cultural shifts, Christians are faced with the challenge of maintaining biblical convictions, especially regarding issues such as sexuality. Over the past few decades, societal attitudes toward sex, marriage, and morality have dramatically changed. Where traditional Christian views on sexuality once held a dominant position, today they are often seen as outdated or irrelevant by many in the broader society. In this chapter, we will explore practical guidance for Christians on how to respond to these cultural shifts while holding fast to biblical truths. Our goal is to equip believers to live faithfully in a world that increasingly rejects God's standard for sexuality and marriage.

1. Understanding the Cultural Shift

The modern world is marked by a cultural revolution, especially regarding sexuality. Issues such as same-sex marriage, transgender rights, and the redefinition of family have become prominent in public discourse. These changes have influenced both secular society and some segments of the Church. As Christians, it is important to understand that these shifts are not merely about changing laws or social norms, but they reflect a deeper spiritual battle—a struggle over truth, identity, and the nature of human beings created in God's image.

In **Romans 12:2**, Paul warns against conforming to the patterns of this world:

"Do not conform to the pattern of this world, but be transformed by the renewing of your mind. Then you will be able to test and approve what God's will is—his good, pleasing, and perfect will."

This scripture encourages Christians to reject the world's values, especially those that conflict with God's design. A failure to recognize the cultural shift and how it contradicts biblical principles can lead to compromise and confusion.

2. Holding to Biblical Convictions

As Christians, our convictions must be rooted in the unchanging truth of God's Word. The Bible teaches a clear and consistent moral framework concerning sexuality, marriage, and gender. Jesus and the apostles upheld the sanctity of marriage between one man and one woman (Matthew 19:4-6), and the New Testament strongly affirms that sexual relations are to take place only within the context of a monogamous, heterosexual marriage (Romans 1:26-27, 1 Corinthians 6:9-11).

The apostle Paul writes in **2 Timothy 3:16-17** that:

"All Scripture is God-breathed and is useful for teaching, rebuking, correcting and training in righteousness, so that the servant of God may be thoroughly equipped for every good work."

Believers must be firmly grounded in the Word of God to navigate the complexities of today's cultural landscape. When faced with societal pressures to accept or endorse ideas that contradict biblical teachings, Christians are called to stand firm in their faith, holding fast to the timeless truth of Scripture.

3. Emphasizing Love and Truth

One of the key tensions Christians must navigate is the balance between loving others and holding to truth. In a culture that often equates love with acceptance of all behavior, Christians must demonstrate that true love includes both compassion and a call to repentance. Jesus exemplified this balance during His earthly ministry. He showed immense compassion to sinners but also called them to repentance, as seen in **John 8:11** when He tells the woman caught in adultery:

"Then neither do I condemn you. Go now and leave your life of sin."

Jesus' love did not condone sin, but rather called for transformation. Similarly, Christians are called to love others without endorsing sinful lifestyles. **Ephesians 4:15** encourages believers to "speak the truth in love," reminding us that truth, when shared in a spirit of love, leads to healing and growth.

While we must stand firm on biblical convictions, we must also show compassion to those who struggle with sexual identity or engage in behaviors contrary to Scripture. **Galatians 6:1** says:

"Brothers and sisters, if someone is caught in a sin, you who live by the Spirit should restore that person gently. But watch yourselves, or you also may be tempted."

This is a call for Christians to engage with others in humility and gentleness, recognizing that everyone is in need of God's grace and mercy. The aim is not to condemn but to restore, pointing people to the transformative power of the gospel.

4. Speaking the Truth with Grace

In an increasingly polarized world, Christians are called to speak the truth boldly but with grace. The apostle Peter wrote in **1 Peter 3:15**:

"But in your hearts revere Christ as Lord. Always be prepared to give an answer to everyone who asks you to give the reason for the hope that you have. But do this with gentleness and respect."

This passage reminds us that while we are called to defend the truth, our defense of biblical convictions must be rooted in gentleness and respect for others. People will not be won over by harshness or condemnation, but through respectful conversations that communicate the love of Christ and the truth of His Word.

When engaging with individuals who disagree with biblical sexual ethics, it is helpful to focus on common ground and to emphasize the hope and transformation found in Christ. Engaging in compassionate conversations can build bridges and open opportunities for sharing the gospel. We should avoid adopting the world's hostile tone in debates about sexuality but instead respond with a Christlike attitude of humility and compassion.

5. Teaching and Equipping the Next Generation

As cultural shifts continue to challenge biblical values, it is crucial to teach and equip the next generation of believers. Christian parents, pastors, and leaders must intentionally instruct young people in the truth of God's Word and the beauty of His design for sexuality. This teaching must be proactive, not reactive, preparing young believers to face the cultural pressures that lie ahead.

Deuteronomy 6:6-7 outlines the importance of teaching God's commandments to the next generation:

"These commandments that I give you today are to be on your hearts. Impress them on your children. Talk about them when you sit at home and when you walk along the road, when you lie down and when you get up."

In a world where the message of sexuality is increasingly distorted, it is vital for Christian leaders to present a biblical vision of marriage, sexuality, and purity. This teaching must be grounded in love, showing how God's design for human sexuality leads to flourishing and true fulfillment. It must also be coupled with practical guidance on how to live out these values in the midst of a culture that often rejects them.

6. The Importance of Prayer and Dependence on God

As Christians seek to navigate these cultural challenges, prayer plays a crucial role. Christians must pray for wisdom, strength, and boldness to stand firm in their faith while demonstrating Christlike love to those around them. **James 1:5** promises:

"If any of you lacks wisdom, let him ask of God, who gives to all liberally and without reproach, and it will be given to him."

Through prayer, Christians can receive the guidance they need to engage with the world in a way that honors God and speaks truthfully to the issues of our day. Christians must also pray for the lost, asking God to soften hearts and open eyes to the transformative power of the gospel.

7. Conclusion: Standing Firm in a Shifting Culture

The cultural shifts regarding sexuality present challenges to Christians, but they also present opportunities to shine the light of truth. By holding firm to biblical convictions, speaking the truth in love, and relying on the power of the Holy Spirit, believers can be faithful witnesses to the gospel in a world that desperately needs it. We must continue to love others, call for repentance, and emphasize the hope of transformation through Christ, trusting that God will use our lives and testimony to bring others to a saving knowledge of Jesus Christ.

In the face of cultural change, let us remember the words of **1 Corinthians 15:58**:

"Therefore, my dear brothers and sisters, stand firm. Let nothing move you. Always give yourselves fully to the work of the Lord, because you know that your labor in the Lord is not in vain."

As Christians, we are called to remain steadfast, grounded in truth, and faithful to the work of God, knowing that our labor in His kingdom will bear fruit.

How to Address Homosexuality with Compassion and Truth

Introduction

In today's world, the issue of homosexuality is one of the most debated and divisive topics within the church and society at large. As Christians, we are called to engage with individuals who identify as homosexual in a way that is both faithful to Scripture and compassionate in nature. The challenge lies in balancing truth with love, as we remain firm in our biblical convictions while offering grace and understanding. This chapter provides practical guidance on how to address homosexuality with compassion and truth, respecting the dignity of individuals while upholding God's Word. It will integrate theological insights and psychological perspectives to offer a holistic approach to this sensitive subject.

---

1. Theological Foundation: Truth in Love

The Bible clearly speaks to the issue of homosexuality, condemning homosexual acts as contrary to God's design for human sexuality (Romans 1:26-27, 1 Corinthians 6:9-10). However, Scripture also calls Christians to love all people, regardless of their sexual orientation, and to offer the message of repentance and transformation through Jesus Christ (John 13:34-35, Matthew 22:37-40).

In **Ephesians 4:15**, Paul encourages believers to "speak the truth in love." This principle applies not only to homosexuality but to all difficult moral issues. The balance of truth and love must govern our conversations with those who identify as homosexual or who struggle with same-sex attraction. While we are called to speak truthfully about God's design for marriage and sexuality, we are also called to do so with kindness, empathy, and respect.

Theological understanding teaches that God's laws are not arbitrary but are given for human flourishing. Marriage, as instituted by God, is a sacred union between one man and one woman (Genesis 2:24, Matthew 19:4-6). Homosexuality, as a deviation from this design, must be addressed from the perspective of redemption, not condemnation. Christ came to save sinners, and this includes those who identify with homosexuality. It is not our role to condemn but to offer the gospel of grace, which transforms lives and renews hearts.

2. *Psychological Perspective: Understanding and Compassion*

Understanding the psychological dynamics of homosexuality is essential for engaging in compassionate conversations. While the Bible presents a moral framework regarding sexual conduct, the reality of human sexuality is complex. For some individuals, same-sex attraction is something they experience involuntarily, and it can be deeply intertwined with their sense of identity, emotions, and experiences. Understanding this complexity can foster empathy and compassion in our interactions.

From a psychological perspective, many individuals with same-sex attraction report that their feelings and desires emerged in early adolescence, and some may experience internal conflict between their faith and their sexual orientation. It's important to approach these conversations with sensitivity, recognizing the struggle that individuals may feel in reconciling their faith and identity.

Christian counselors often approach this issue with a commitment to helping individuals navigate their desires while emphasizing the importance of a relationship with Christ. **2 Corinthians 5:17** declares that "if anyone is in Christ, the new creation has come: The old has gone, the new is here!" This verse affirms the transformative power of the gospel, which is able to renew not only a person's spiritual condition but their emotional and psychological life as well.

In engaging individuals who struggle with same-sex attraction, it is crucial to respect their autonomy while offering the love of Christ, which is both redemptive and empowering. It is essential to approach them not with judgment but with a desire to understand their experiences, listening to their struggles, and offering a safe space for dialogue. Empathy is key in acknowledging that the psychological and emotional journey toward healing and wholeness is a process that can take time.

3. Compassionate Communication: Speaking the Truth in Love

To speak the truth in love means that we approach the subject of homosexuality with respect and tenderness. It involves affirming the dignity of the individual, acknowledging their worth as created in the image of God (Genesis 1:27), and engaging with them in a way that demonstrates Christ's love and compassion. We must communicate that while we hold to biblical convictions regarding marriage and sexuality, we are committed to loving people and sharing the hope of transformation through Jesus Christ.

Here are several key principles for compassionate communication:

- **Affirm the Person's Dignity**: Every person is made in the image of God and is valuable in His sight (Psalm 139:14). Our words should always reflect this truth. Before addressing the issue of homosexuality, we should seek to affirm the person's inherent worth and dignity.
- **Be Humble and Non-Judgmental**: It is easy to fall into a self-righteous attitude when dealing with issues of sin. However, Jesus made it clear that we are all sinners in need of His grace (Romans 3:23). We must approach those with whom we disagree with humility, recognizing that we too have fallen short of God's glory.
- **Focus on the Gospel**: The message of the gospel is one of transformation and redemption. Jesus did not come to condemn the world but to save it (John 3:17). Our message should always be focused on the good news of Christ's ability to forgive sins and transform lives, including those struggling with same-sex attraction. We should never present the gospel as a "fix" for homosexual feelings but rather as an invitation into a relationship with Christ, where all desires and identities are made new.
- **Address the Root Cause**: The ultimate issue is not merely behavior, but the heart's condition. Jesus made it clear that the heart is the seat of sin (Matthew 15:19), and sexual sin is often a symptom of deeper emotional or relational needs. Christians should encourage individuals to seek healing not only in their sexual behavior but in their hearts and relationships with God.

---

4. Creating a Safe Environment for Dialogue

Creating a safe space for individuals to share their stories is essential in engaging with them effectively. People who identify as homosexual may have experienced rejection or condemnation from others, and it is crucial that the Church becomes a place where they feel heard and understood. This is especially important in our current cultural climate, where many people feel alienated from the Church due to perceived hostility toward LGBTQ+ individuals.

Creating a safe environment includes:

- **Active Listening**: When someone shares their struggles or their story, it is essential to listen actively, without interruption or judgment. Listening allows you to understand the person's experience and express compassion and care.
- **Avoiding Stereotyping**: Homosexuality is a deeply personal and complex issue. Rather than making assumptions about someone's life or experiences, it is vital to ask questions and engage with them individually.
- **Encouraging Personal Growth**: Rather than focusing solely on their sexuality, encourage individuals to grow in their faith, to seek emotional and spiritual healing, and to develop a stronger relationship with Christ. Every person's journey will be unique, and there is no one-size-fits-all answer.

5. The Goal: Restoration and Transformation

The goal of addressing homosexuality is not to win an argument or enforce conformity to a set of moral standards but to point individuals toward the hope of restoration through

Christ. **1 Corinthians 6:9-11** provides an example of transformation through the gospel:

"Do not be deceived: Neither the sexually immoral nor idolaters nor adulterers nor men who have sex with men...will inherit the kingdom of God. And that is what some of you were. But you were washed, you were sanctified, you were justified in the name of the Lord Jesus Christ and by the Spirit of our God."

This passage highlights the transformative power of the gospel. Just as Christ offers forgiveness for all sins, He also offers the grace to overcome them. Homosexuality, like other sins, can be overcome through the power of the Holy Spirit. As Christians, we must offer this hope—encouraging individuals to trust in Christ's ability to bring about real change.

Conclusion

Addressing homosexuality with compassion and truth is one of the most important and challenging tasks for the Church today. It requires us to hold fast to biblical truth while extending grace, understanding, and love to those who identify as homosexual or struggle with same-sex attraction. By grounding our response in theological and psychological perspectives, we can offer the hope of transformation, point individuals to the gospel, and create an environment where people can experience the life-changing love of Jesus Christ. As we engage with those who disagree or struggle with biblical teachings on sexuality, let us reflect Christ's love, truth, and grace—always speaking the truth in love, with the aim of restoration and healing.

Living as Salt and Light: Reflecting Christ's Character with Truth and Compassion

Introduction

As Christians, we are called to be both salt and light in a world that often stands in contrast to God's truths. Jesus' teachings, especially His call to be salt and light, carry a dual responsibility for believers: to preserve and illuminate the world around us while upholding God's truth and embodying His compassion. Living as salt and light means reflecting Christ's character, being agents of change and transformation, and engaging the world in a way that points others to Him. In this chapter, we will explore how Christians can balance truth with compassion, emphasizing the importance of living with integrity, grace, and love in our interactions with others.

1. The Call to Be Salt and Light

In **Matthew 5:13-16**, Jesus calls His followers to be salt and light:

- **Salt**: "You are the salt of the earth. But if the salt loses its saltiness, how can it be made salty again? It is no longer good for anything, except to be thrown out and trampled by men" (Matthew 5:13).
- **Light**: "You are the light of the world. A city on a hill cannot be hidden. Neither do people light a lamp and put it under a bowl. Instead, they put it on its stand, and it gives light to everyone in the house" (Matthew 5:14-15).

Salt has multiple functions, primarily preserving and seasoning. In the context of our Christian walk, salt symbolizes our role in preserving the moral and spiritual health of the world. As Christians, we are to influence society, upholding and promoting God's standards of truth, justice, and love. Light, on the other hand, represents the gospel of Christ, which shines into a world of darkness, guiding people to truth, hope, and salvation.

Jesus not only calls His followers to be different from the world but to make a visible difference. Our character, conduct, and words should reflect the light of Christ. **1 Peter 2:9** states, "But you are a chosen people, a royal priesthood, a holy nation, God's special possession, that you may declare the praises of him who called you out of darkness into his wonderful light."

2. Balancing Truth and Compassion

To live as salt and light, we must learn to balance the seemingly opposing forces of truth and compassion. The truth of God's Word does not change based on cultural shifts, and it is our duty as Christians to stand firm on biblical principles. However, the manner in which we present these truths must always be tempered with compassion, humility, and a desire for reconciliation. **Ephesians 4:15** instructs believers to "speak the truth in love," highlighting the necessity of balancing doctrinal clarity with relational warmth.

While truth is non-negotiable, how we communicate that truth matters greatly. The gospel is offensive to the sinful nature of humanity (1 Corinthians 1:18), yet we must never use it as a weapon to harm or belittle others. Compassionate engagement means meeting people where they are, understanding their struggles, and offering them the hope of transformation through Christ.

- **Jesus' Example**: Jesus perfectly modeled the balance of truth and compassion. He did not shy away from confronting sin but always did so with a heart for redemption. Consider His interaction with the woman caught in adultery (John 8:1-11). Jesus exposed the sin, saying, "Go now and leave your life of sin," but He also extended grace and mercy, preventing her from being condemned by others. His gentle rebuke, combined with His compassionate response, provided a model for how Christians should respond to those caught in sin.
- **The Apostle Paul's Example**: Paul, too, exemplified this balance. He rebuked the Corinthian church for tolerating immorality (1 Corinthians 5), but he also wrote tenderly to restore a fallen brother (2 Corinthians 2:5-8). Paul's approach was always to correct with the aim of restoration, ensuring that his words were not merely harsh judgments but calls to repentance and hope.

---

3. Reflecting Christ's Character in a Divided World

As believers, we are to be a reflection of Christ's character. The world today is full of division, especially when it comes to moral issues such as sexuality. Christians are not immune to these cultural divisions, but we are called to rise above them. Our interactions must not mirror the bitterness and hostility of the world but reflect Christ's love, grace, and truth.

- **Humility**: Christ, though the Son of God, came in humility, serving and loving those who were often marginalized (Matthew 20:28). In contrast to the pride and self-righteousness of the Pharisees, He demonstrated what true humility looks like—recognizing His own sinfulness and the need for God's mercy. Christians today should approach the topic of homosexuality—and all sensitive issues—with humility, remembering that we, too, are sinners saved by grace (Romans 3:23-24).

- **Grace and Mercy**: God's grace is immeasurable, and He offers forgiveness to all who repent, regardless of their sin. We should extend the same grace to others. **Romans 5:8** tells us, "But God demonstrates his own love for us in this: While we were still sinners, Christ died for us." This is the heart of the gospel message: that God's love is unmerited, and His mercy is abundant. As we share the gospel with others, we must remember that grace is offered first and foremost, followed by the call to repentance.

- **Patience**: Christians must practice patience with others, especially those who are struggling with sin. **2 Peter 3:9** tells us that God is "not wanting anyone to perish, but everyone to come to repentance." Patience with others gives space for the Holy Spirit to work in their hearts, and it demonstrates the same patience that God has shown toward us.

---

4. How to Engage in Difficult Conversations

It is important to recognize that living as salt and light will sometimes require difficult conversations. As Christians, we should be prepared to lovingly address sensitive topics, including homosexuality, in ways that honor God and demonstrate the love of Christ.

- **Be Prepared with the Truth**: As believers, we should be well-versed in Scripture and prepared to give an answer for the hope we have in Christ (1 Peter 3:15). When addressing issues like homosexuality, it is important to be clear about what Scripture teaches while remembering the heart of God, which desires redemption for all people.
- **Listen First**: Before speaking, listen. Understanding the experiences and struggles of those with whom we are engaging will help us to speak with empathy and discernment. Listening is often the first step toward building a relationship of trust, which is essential for sharing the gospel.
- **Avoid Arguing or Condemning**: Our goal should never be to win an argument but to win souls for Christ. Avoid making the conversation about proving someone wrong and instead focus on the gospel message—the hope of transformation and redemption that is found in Jesus alone.
- **Show Compassion**: Always aim to connect on a personal level, showing genuine care and concern for the person's well-being. Love and compassion will often open doors for the gospel to be heard.

5. Living Out the Call to Be Salt and Light

To truly live as salt and light, Christians must embody Christ's character in all areas of life. This includes how we respond to sin, how we engage with others, and how we represent Christ's kingdom on earth. In a world that desperately needs both truth and love, we are called to be the conduits through which God's grace and truth flow.

Matthew 5:16 says, "Let your light shine before others, that they may see your good deeds and glorify your Father in heaven." Our lives should be a testament to God's transforming power. When we live out our faith with authenticity, humility, and compassion, we bring glory to God and demonstrate the beauty of the gospel to a watching world.

Conclusion

Living as salt and light is not just about what we do, but about who we are in Christ. As Christians, we are called to reflect Christ's character, balancing truth with compassion in our interactions with others. We must be faithful to God's Word, speaking His truth boldly, yet doing so with love, grace, and respect. This approach not only honors God but also opens the door for transformation, drawing others to the hope of salvation that is found in Jesus Christ alone.

CONCLUSION

Summarizing Jesus' Position on Homosexuality

In exploring the issue of homosexuality through the lens of Scripture and the teachings of Jesus, it becomes clear that Jesus upheld a vision of marriage and sexuality that does not align with homosexual acts. While Jesus did not directly address homosexuality in the explicit terms that some might expect, His foundational teachings on marriage, human sexuality, and sin provide a clear framework for understanding His stance.

1. The Creation Mandate and Marriage

Jesus' teachings in **Matthew 19:4-6** reaffirm the creation narrative from **Genesis 2:24**, where He declares that marriage is between one man and one woman: "For this reason a man will leave his father and mother and be united to his wife, and the two will become one flesh." Jesus upholds this divine design, emphasizing the complementary roles of man and woman in marriage. This vision of marriage as between one man and one woman lays the foundation for biblical sexual ethics, which does not accommodate same-sex relationships.

2. The Consistency of Biblical Sexual Morality

While Jesus did not speak explicitly to homosexuality, His broader teachings on sexual morality are unequivocal. In

Matthew 5:27-28, He raises the bar for sexual purity, condemning lust and emphasizing that even looking at someone with lustful intent is sinful. This emphasis on the sanctity and purity of human sexuality, as designed by God, supports the biblical stance that sexual relationships should occur within the covenant of marriage between a man and a woman. Homosexual acts, as contrary to this design, fall outside of God's intended order.

3. Jesus' Ministry and Compassion

Jesus' ministry was one of compassion, grace, and an invitation to repentance. He called all people, including those living in sin, to follow Him and experience the transformative power of God's love. **John 8:11**, where Jesus tells the woman caught in adultery to "go and sin no more," exemplifies His willingness to offer grace while also calling for repentance. This pattern applies to all sinners, including those engaging in homosexual acts. Jesus' love for individuals does not mean that He condones sin but rather invites sinners to repentance and transformation.

4. The Apostolic Affirmation of Jesus' Teachings

While Jesus did not specifically address homosexuality, the apostles, who were inspired by the Holy Spirit, upheld Jesus' teachings on marriage and sexuality. In **Romans 1:26-27, 1 Corinthians 6:9-11**, and **1 Timothy 1:9-10**, the apostolic writings reinforce the biblical stance that homosexual acts are sinful and contrary to God's design. These teachings reflect the authority of Jesus and His call to righteousness. As the apostles were Jesus' authoritative representatives, their teachings serve as a direct continuation of His will and purpose.

5. *The Call to Repentance and Transformation*

Jesus' message was one of redemption and transformation for all people. In **Luke 5:32**, He says, "I have not come to call the righteous, but sinners to repentance." His ministry was not about condemnation but about offering a path to salvation for all who would turn from sin and follow Him. Homosexuality, like all sin, falls under the need for repentance and the transformative power of the gospel.

In conclusion, while Jesus did not address homosexuality in the same terms as modern discussions, His teachings on marriage, sexuality, and sin provide a clear framework for understanding His position. Jesus affirmed God's design for marriage as being between one man and one woman, and He consistently upheld the sanctity of human sexuality. As His followers, Christians are called to reflect His love, offering grace and compassion while remaining faithful to His teachings on sexual morality. Ultimately, Jesus' call to repentance and transformation is extended to all, including those who engage in homosexual acts, offering the hope of forgiveness and new life through faith in Him.

The Call to Uphold Biblical Teachings

As followers of Christ, all believers are called to uphold the truth of Scripture as the inspired Word of God, which holds ultimate authority in guiding our lives, decisions, and actions. Throughout the Bible, we see the consistent theme that God's Word is the standard for how we should live and navigate the complexities of life. From the teachings of Jesus to the apostolic writings, the Bible provides a firm foundation for understanding God's will on moral issues, including human sexuality.

1. The Authority of Scripture

In **2 Timothy 3:16-17**, Paul reminds believers that "all Scripture is breathed out by God and profitable for teaching, for reproof, for correction, and for training in righteousness, that the man of God may be complete, equipped for every good work." This passage underscores that Scripture is divinely inspired and serves as the authoritative guide for Christian living. The teachings in both the Old and New Testaments are not subject to cultural trends or changing societal norms. Rather, they reflect God's eternal truth, which remains relevant and applicable for believers today.

2. Jesus' Affirmation of Scripture

Jesus Himself consistently affirmed the authority of Scripture. In **Matthew 5:17-18**, He states, "Do not think that I have come to abolish the Law or the Prophets; I have not come to abolish them but to fulfill them." Jesus upheld the authority of the Scriptures, pointing to their fulfillment in His life and teachings. As His followers, we are called to honor God's Word as the standard for our moral and ethical conduct. Jesus did not diminish the significance of the law but highlighted its deeper fulfillment through His own obedience and the call to live according to God's righteous standards.

3. The Role of Scripture in the Christian Life

Believers are commanded to let God's Word dwell richly in their hearts, as we see in **Colossians 3:16**: "Let the word of

Christ dwell in you richly, teaching and admonishing one another in all wisdom, singing psalms and hymns and spiritual songs, with thankfulness in your hearts to God." This passage speaks to the central role of Scripture in shaping our thoughts, actions, and interactions with others. By immersing ourselves in the truth of God's Word, we are equipped to uphold His standards in all aspects of life, including issues like human sexuality.

4. Upholding Biblical Truth in a Changing World

In a society where cultural norms continue to shift, believers are called to stand firm on the truths of Scripture. **Romans 12:2** urges believers, "Do not be conformed to this world, but be transformed by the renewal of your mind, that by testing you may discern what is the will of God, what is good and acceptable and perfect." The world may attempt to redefine marriage, sexuality, and morality, but Christians are called to renew their minds in God's Word and hold fast to the eternal truths it reveals. Upholding biblical teachings means resisting the pressures of a culture that seeks to normalize behaviors that go against God's design.

5. The Call to Live According to Scripture

As believers, it is not enough to merely profess faith in Jesus. We are called to live out our faith by aligning our lives with the teachings of Scripture. **James 1:22** exhorts, "But be doers of the word, and not hearers only, deceiving yourselves." This means that we must not only acknowledge the truth of God's Word but also apply it to our lives, living in obedience to His commands. This applies to all areas of life, including how we view and engage with issues of sexuality, marriage, and morality. By upholding biblical teachings, believers serve as witnesses to the world of God's unchanging truth and His plan for human flourishing.

6. Compassionate Truth-Telling

Upholding biblical truth does not mean we abandon compassion. In fact, it is through holding fast to God's Word that we are equipped to engage with the world in love and truth. Jesus exemplified this balance, offering grace to sinners while calling them to repentance. **John 1:14** tells us, "And the Word became flesh and dwelt among us, and we have seen His glory, glory as of the only Son from the Father, full of grace and truth." As followers of Christ, we are called to do the same—speaking truth with compassion, inviting others to experience the transformative power of the gospel while remaining faithful to God's Word.

In conclusion, the call to uphold biblical teachings is a call to honor God's Word as the final authority on matters of faith, morality, and human sexuality. As believers, we are entrusted with the responsibility to live out these teachings in our lives, to resist cultural pressures that seek to redefine God's design, and to offer both truth and grace to a world in need of redemption. By doing so, we reflect Christ's character and bear witness to the hope of transformation through the gospel.

An Invitation to Seek Transformation

As we conclude this exploration of Jesus' teachings and biblical sexuality, it is crucial to remember that the message of Christ is ultimately one of transformation. Jesus did not come merely to offer moral teachings or ethical guidelines, but to invite all people to experience a profound change of heart and life through the power of the gospel. This transformation is available to everyone, regardless of their past, their struggles, or their sins. The call to follow Jesus is a call to embrace a new life—one that reflects His righteousness, truth, and love.

1. The Transforming Power of the Gospel

The gospel message is not just about knowing what is right; it is about being made right with God through Jesus Christ. **2 Corinthians 5:17** reminds us that, "If anyone is in Christ, he is a new creation. The old has passed away; behold, the new has come." This verse encapsulates the essence of the Christian life: through faith in Jesus, we are transformed, leaving behind our old sinful ways and walking in the newness of life He offers. This transformation affects every area of our lives, including how we view and approach issues such as sexuality and relationships.

2. Jesus' Call to Repentance and Faith

Throughout His ministry, Jesus called people to repentance and faith. **Mark 1:15** records Jesus' proclamation: "The time is fulfilled, and the kingdom of God is at hand; repent and believe in the gospel." Repentance involves turning away from sin and turning toward God in faith. This is not a mere outward change, but a radical shift in our hearts and minds, empowered by the Holy Spirit. In **Luke 5:32**, Jesus stated, "I have not come to call the righteous but sinners to repentance." No one is beyond the reach of Jesus' transformative grace. His invitation to follow Him is open to all, and it is through repentance and faith in Him that we are made new.

3. The Process of Sanctification

Transformation in Christ is a lifelong process known as sanctification, where believers are continually conformed to the image of Christ. **Romans 8:29** tells us that God "predestined us to be conformed to the image of His Son." This process involves growing in holiness, reflecting God's righteousness in our thoughts, actions, and relationships. Sanctification requires not only a change in behavior but a deep renewal of the mind and heart, as described in **Romans 12:2**: "Do not be conformed to this world, but be transformed by the renewal of your mind, that by testing you may discern what is the will of God, what is good and acceptable and perfect."

4. The Hope of Redemption

No matter where you are in your journey, there is always hope in Christ. The gospel is good news because it offers redemption, not based on our merit but on the grace of God. **1 Corinthians 6:9-11** highlights this hope: "Or do you not know that the unrighteous will not inherit the kingdom of God? Do not be deceived: neither the sexually immoral, nor idolaters, nor adulterers, nor men who practice homosexuality... will inherit the kingdom of God. And such were some of you. But you were washed, you were sanctified, you were justified in the name of the Lord Jesus Christ and by the Spirit of our God." These verses remind us that no one is beyond the transforming power of God. The very people who once lived in sin are now made new through the grace of Christ.

5. The Call to Follow Jesus in Righteousness and Truth

Jesus' call to transformation is also a call to live in righteousness and truth. Following Jesus means walking in His ways, living according to the standards He set forth, and reflecting His holiness. **1 John 2:6** says, "Whoever says he abides in Him ought to walk in the same way in which He walked." Jesus exemplified perfect holiness, love, and truth, and we are called to follow His example, empowered by the Holy Spirit. This means living lives that honor God in every area, including our sexuality, relationships, and interactions with others.

6. A Lifelong Journey of Transformation

The call to transformation is not a one-time event but a lifelong journey. As we grow in our relationship with Christ, we learn more about His heart, His will, and His plan for our lives. The Holy Spirit works in us to cultivate the fruits of the Spirit, which are evidence of our transformation. **Galatians 5:22-23** speaks of these fruits: "But the fruit of the Spirit is love, joy, peace, forbearance, kindness, goodness, faithfulness, gentleness and self-control." These qualities are not natural to us but are the result of the Holy Spirit's work in us as we submit to God's Word and allow it to transform us.

Invitation to Transformation

Jesus' invitation to transformation is open to all, no matter the struggles or sins we face. He calls us to repentance, to believe in the gospel, and to follow Him in righteousness and truth.

Through His grace, we are made new, and through His Spirit, we are empowered to live lives that reflect His holiness. The message of the gospel is one of hope, offering redemption and a new beginning. It is a call to leave behind our old ways, to be renewed in mind and spirit, and to live according to the will of God.

Will you accept this invitation to transformation? Will you follow Jesus in righteousness and truth, allowing His love and grace to change you from the inside out? The path of transformation begins with a simple yet profound step—repentance and faith in Jesus Christ. As you follow Him, He will continue to shape you, leading you to a life of greater holiness and joy, living in accordance with His divine purpose.

www.ingramcontent.com/pod-product-compliance
Lightning Source LLC
Chambersburg PA
CBHW060914140726
47996CB00001B/245